WHAT ARE MY CHANCES?

BOOK A

Albert P. Shulte
Oakland Schools, Pontiac, Michigan

Stuart A. Choate
Pontiac Schools, Pontiac, Michigan

CREATIVE PUBLICATIONS

PALO ALTO, CA 94303

Project Editor
Virginia Thompson

Artwork by Susan Jaekel

© 1977 Creative Publications, Inc.
P. O. Box 10328
Palo Alto, California 94303
Printed in U.S.A.

ISBN: 0-88488-082-6

3 4 5 6 7 8 9 10 . 8 9 8 7 6 5 4

CONTENTS

INTRODUCTION

The study of probability leads to a different kind of mathematical thinking. Probabilities do not furnish absolute answers to specific questions; they suggest what to expect on the average, in the long run—or theoretically. Experience with probability helps to develop a perspective on real-life situations for which the answers are not known or will not be known until after a decision has been made. Because this mode of thinking may be new to your students, you may find that the study of probability evokes surprising responses from them. Some of the better students may experience trouble when faced with problems that do not have absolute solutions, while some of the poorer students may find these new concepts exciting.

At all levels, the subject of probability is best introduced and developed on an intuitive basis through hands-on activities and experiments. The most common lesson sequence used in this book is:

Thinking about a situation or experiment;

Predicting the possible results—theoretically, intuitively, or by taking a small sample;

Performing the experiment or taking a survey;

Comparing the experimental results to the predictions.

The main concepts covered in this book are: organized listing; the meaning of probability; how to calculate and express probabilities in fraction, decimal, and per cent form; the Law of Large Numbers; and the use of surveys to predict future situations and results for larger groups. These concepts are developed in a spiral manner throughout the 73 activities.

To assist in planning, teacher notes and notes regarding the materials have been included following this introduction. The teacher notes are meant to supply sufficient information so that, even with little or no previous experience in teaching probability, you will find the activities easy and enjoyable to use. In the teacher notes for each activity, the main concepts and skills to be developed in that lesson are listed first in boldface type. They are followed by suggestions for explaining new concepts and by notes regarding the details of the activity. Particular lessons are specified as mini-lessons in the teacher notes as well as on the activity pages, when new material can best be presented in discussion form to small groups or the whole class. A solution key is found at the back of the book.

MATERIALS

The materials for each activity are listed on the bottom of the activity page. They consist primarily of objects that can be collected easily from the classroom or home. All of the materials used are listed below. Special notes follow for those marked with an asterisk.

almanac or encyclopedia

books (library)

coins

crayons

graph paper

newspapers (including stock market page)

paper

pencils

pens

regular 52-card deck of playing cards

TV guides

colored marbles or other counters*

containers such as paper sacks or boxes*

polyhedra dice*

regular dice*

special cards*

spinners

thumbtacks*

toothpaste caps*

Colored marbles and containers (Activities 30, 31, 32, 48, 49, 51, 63, 68, 72). These activities consist of drawing marbles or cubes from a container. In all of the activities, any objects or counters may be substituted for the marbles or cubes as long as they are identical to touch and the appropriate colors. Also, any can, box, or sack may be used for the container as long as the students cannot see what they are drawing. The maximum number of marbles required at one time is 6 blue, 4 green, 10 red, and 6 yellow marbles, except for Activity 72 which requires 75 blue and 75 red marbles. In the latter case, you may want to use colored tagboard, or construction paper squares.

Polyhedra dice (Activities 8, 37, 38, 59, 65). Activity 37 requires 2 octahedra dice for each student or group of students. The other activities involving polyhedra dice require only one die for each student or group of students. Creative Publications sells sets of polyhedra dice consisting of a tetrahedron, cube (regular die), octahedron, dodecahedron, and icosahedron.

Regular dice (Activities 7, 9–10, 13, 26–29, 40, 44, 58, 70, 73). The maximum number of dice needed is 3 for every student or group of students. In Activity 20 the dice need to be different colors.

Special cards (Activities 5, 22). Activity 5 requires a set of 8 red, 8 yellow, and 8 blue cards for each student or group of students. They can be made from tagboard or construction paper.

Activity 22 requires a set of cards numbered from 1 to 10 for each student or group of students. Use the numbered cards from a playing-card deck (with ace = 1) or make your own—or have the students make their own—from tagboard or other cardboard. Construction paper will not work in this case because the cards must be stiff enough to withstand frequent shuffling for this activity.

Thumbtacks (Activity 19). Each pair or group of students working on the lesson at the same time will need 10 identical thumbtacks. If you plan to have the students combine their results, all of the thumbtacks should be identical.

Toothpaste caps (Activity 45). Each student or group of students will need one toothpaste cap. If the students plan to combine their results all of the caps should be identical.

Spinners (Activities 2–4, 9, 10, 13, 17, 46–47, 66). Both numbered and blank spinner sets are available from Creative Publications. Directions for making your own spinners follow.

On page 4, there are two spinner and pointer patterns. The marks on the circumferences indicate divisions for 3, 4, 5, 6, 8, 10, and 12 equal parts. Look at the sketches in specific lessons to see which faces you will need. The inner circle can be used to make one spinner for two sets of divisions. For example, the spinner below shows 5 equal parts marked on the inner circle and 10 marked on the outer circle.

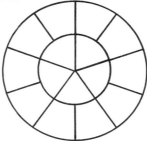

To make your own spinners, or to have the students make their own, follow the directions below.

1. Duplicate or draw the basic spinner pattern on tagboard.
2. Cut out the square. Punch a hole in the center.
3. Draw and color or number the appropriate divisions.
4. Mount the pointer on the spinner using a brad (paper fastener) as illustrated. First put on a washer, then the pointer, then the second washer, and finally the spinner face. (If regular washers are not available, pieces of 1 cm square tagboard can be substituted.)
5. Bend the ends of the brad flat and tape them in place.
6. To insure a flat bottom for the spinner, cut out a second square with a circular hole the size of the inner circle on the pattern. Glue or tape this square to the bottom of the spinner as illustrated.
7. To spin, hold firmly in two corners.

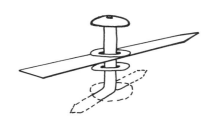

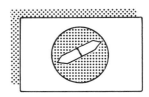

Note. All spinner activities can be replaced by activities involving drawing marbles or color cubes from a container with replacement. You will need the same proportion of cubes for each color or number as the proportion of area of each on the spinner. For example, for Activity 2, you would need 2 red, 1 green, and 3 yellow cubes. Return the cube after each draw and mix the cubes thoroughly before the next draw.

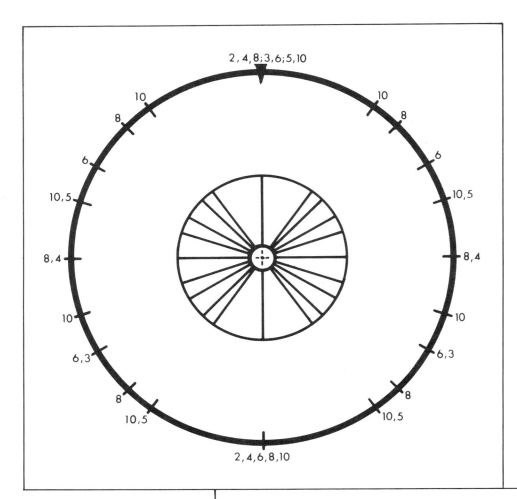

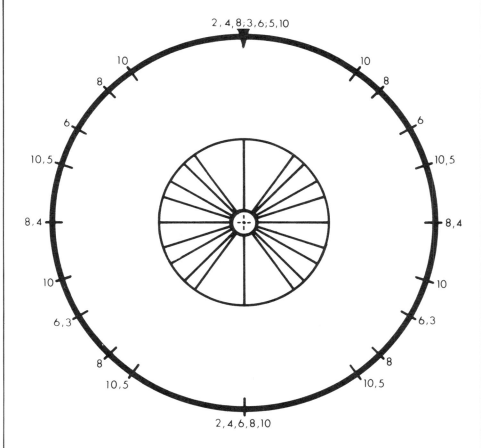

TEACHER NOTES

1 HEADS OR TAILS
Predicting, experimenting, and interpreting results.

The students should be able to estimate that about half the tosses of a coin will result in heads. The experiment will help them realize that the result of *exactly* half heads is an unusual event. Accumulating the data for the whole class will show that increasing the sample size increases the chance that the experimental results will more closely approximate the theoretical ratio.

2 YELLOW-RED-GREEN
Performing an experiment to test the ability of predicting individual outcomes on spinners.

The students are asked to predict individual outcomes and record their successes for two games. Although the spinner has more yellow area, in the first game, many students will not use this information in their predictions, even when they can verbalize it. In the second game, the spinner is used such that the possible outcomes are equally likely. In this case, there is no basis for predicting one outcome over another. The students should discuss the two experimental situations and how their differences affect the games.

Directions for making spinners are given on page 3. Directions for using color cubes in place of the spinner are given at the bottom of the activity page.

3 SPIN A COLOR
Predicting, experimenting, and interpreting results.

The students use a spinner with equally likely outcomes as a probability model here. The emphasis in this lesson is on considering what happens—or what you would expect to happen—*on the average,* rather than on the results of individual events. This distinction illustrates the essence of what probability can and cannot do: Probabilities tell what can be expected from a particular situation or experiment in the long run—not exactly what will happen on a given trial or few trials.

Accumulating the results for the whole class will show again that a larger sample size produces experimental results that approximate the theoretical results more closely. The students will need to know how to keep a tally to do this page. Directions for making spinners are given on page 3. Directions for using color cubes in place of the spinner are given at the bottom of the activity page.

4 THINKING ABOUT MORE SPINNERS
Predicting expected numbers of outcomes.

The students predict the number of times they expect each outcome to occur in 100 spins for three different spinner models. In each case, the possible outcomes are equally likely. As an extension, the students are asked to perform the experiments and compare their results to their predictions. Directions for making spinners are given on page 3. Again, color cubes can be used in place of the spinners.

5 GUESSING COLORS
Predicting and listing the possible outcomes of the situation.

This activity provides preliminary work with permutations (ordered arrangements), with organized listing of possible outcomes, and with separating possible outcomes into desired outcomes (favorable outcomes) and undesired outcomes (unfavorable outcomes). These important concepts are basic to the study of probability.

6 HOW'S YOUR POP?
Listing possible outcomes, predicting, experimenting, and interpreting results.

This taste-testing experiment is fun for students and easy to carry out in a class.
One way to do it easily is to pre-pour the colas into small cups labeled A, B, and C. (You will need a set of samples for each student participating in the experiment.) The students taste from each and write down their predictions.

Groups vary widely in their ability to distinguish the colas. *Individuals* may actually be able to tell the differences without the group being able to score much above the chance level. For a group of individuals, the expected number to guess all three colas right by chance is n/6. For a class of 30, if the number getting all three colas right is more than 9 or 10 students the group can be said statistically to have the ability to distinguish among the colas.

Three varieties of chewing gum can be used in place of the colas for this activity.

7 ROLLING A DIE
Experimenting with a die and interpreting the results.

This activity builds on Activity 1, Heads or Tails, and Activity 3, Spin a Color, and reinforces the same goals. Accumulation of results for the whole class is useful.

Having completed this activity, the students will have been introduced to three common probability models: coins, spinners, and dice.

8 ROLLING THE DODECAHEDRON
Performing an experiment and recording the results.

The dodecahedron makes a good die that tumbles well. Dodecahedron dice were used early in history. In fact, all of the five regular polyhedra (the cube, octahedron, tetrahedron, dodecahedron, and icosahedron) can be used as dice.

9 PROBABILITY *Mini-Lesson*
Defining the term probability and determing probabilities of simple events.

The term *probability* is introduced for the first time. The students should be able to draw on their experiences from the previous activities to answer the questions here.

This activity is best presented as a discussion lesson to a small group or the whole class followed by Activity 10 to reinforce the new concepts. Encourage the students to contribute as much of the information as possible in the discussion; allow them time to discuss the questions before you help them with answers.

10 FINDING PROBABILITIES
Listing events and determining probabilities of simple events.

The students determine probabilities for situations involving one die and spinners by listing and counting outcomes. Exercises 1 and 3 include situations in which some outcomes are more likely than others.

This activity is the follow-up for Activity 9.

11 SHORTCUTS FOR WRITING PROBABILITIES *Mini-Lesson*
Writing statements of probabilities in symbolic form; examining probability statements written in symbolic form and writing them in English.

In this activity, the students practice examining a verbal or written statement of probability and writing it in functional notation, that is, in the form Pr(E) where E is the desired event—the one that is being asked about. They also practice translating the symbolic form into English statements. They are introduced to probabilities expressed in decimal and per cent form. Ask the students the fractional equivalents of these figures and how they relate to the definition of probability.

This activity is best presented as a mini-lesson to small groups or the whole class.

12 ARE YOU CERTAIN? OR ARE YOU IMPOSSIBLE? *Mini-Lesson*
Labeling events as certain, possible, and impossible.

The purpose of this activity is to establish that all events can be categorized as impossible, possible, or certain.

This activity is best presented as a discussion lesson to small groups or the whole class. Encourage the students to contribute as much of the information as possible.

13 SOME PROBABILITIES
Determining probabilities of simple and compound events.

This activity provides additional practice in determining probabilities of simple and compound events. The students are also introduced through the exercises to the rules that are given in the next lesson. Remind the students that the probability of an event is

$$\frac{\text{the number of ways it can happen}}{\text{the total number of things that could happen}}$$

You might wish to have the students work in pairs or small groups on the problems and then discuss their results with you or an aide.

14 SOME PROBABILITY RULES *Mini-Lesson*
A reference page listing important principles of probability.

Treat this activity as a discussion lesson to formally establish the basic rules of probability:

Pr(impossible event) = 0;
Pr(certain event) = 1;
All other probabilities are between 0 and 1.
Pr(something happens) + Pr(that thing does not happen) = 1.

15 PROBABILITY OF NOT GETTING SOMETHING
Determining the probability of an event not occurring given the probability of its occurrence.

Practice in applying the principles:

Pr(not E) = 1 - Pr(E);
Pr(E) = 1 - Pr(not E).

These principles are based on the last rule given in lesson 14: Pr(E) + Pr(not E) = 1. This fact should be emphasized in the discussion of the lesson.

16 SOME SPORTS QUESTIONS
Determining probabilities in applied real-life situations.

This activity relates probability to sports—a part of the real world that interests many students. Here we are using past records, or what are called empirical probabilities, to predict future events. All of the problems can be solved using the probability rule: Pr(not E) = 1 - Pr(E).

17   SPIN A NUMBER
Predicting outcomes, performing an experiment, and comparing experimental results with a prediction.

The students should have enough experience to predict that each number should come up 10 out of 100 times. When written as a fraction (10/100 or 1/10), this statement expresses the theoretical probability of the occurrence of each number on this particular spinner.

Encourage the students to discuss why their experimental results are not exactly the same as what they expected. Ask what will happen if they combine their results. Then have them combine their results and compare the combined results with what they originally expected. The discussion should elicit the point that when we say that an event has the theoretical probability of, for example, 1/10, we mean that when we consider many cases, we expect that event will occur about 1/10 of the time. It does *not* mean that we will find that that event occurs *exactly* 1/10 of the time for each experiment we do.

Directions for making the spinners are given on page 3. Again, color cubes can be used in place of the spinner.

18   COUNTING WORD LENGTHS
Performing an experiment, defining experimental probability, determining experimental probabilities, and repeating the experiment to check for consistency.

This is the students' introduction to determining empirical or experimental probabilities, probabilities based on an experiment, not on a theoretical model. By performing the experiment twice, the students have the opportunity to see if their results tend to be stable and thus useful for future predictions. Accumulating the results for the whole class will provide a fair approximation of the distribution of word lengths in the English language.

19   FINDING PROBABILITIES FROM EXPERIMENTS
Finding experimental probabilities for a situation in which there is no known model.

Thumbtacks are good, readily available objects for a probability experiment in which there are no known theoretical probabilities. Since the probabilities will vary if the base or shaft of the thumbtacks are different, all the thumbtacks tossed should be the same type. As with other experiments it is helpful and informative to accumulate the results for the whole class to obtain more accurate experimental probabilities to make future predictions.

20   CARS, CARS, CARS
Making a survey, writing experimental probabilities, and repeating the survey to check for consistency.

This experiment works best if the school is located on a busy street. If it is not, careful planning for proper supervision will be necessary. Before beginning the project, the students should consider such problems as what to do if they see a two-color car or a VW van with a camper inside. Such a discussion will emphasize some of the problems that occur when making up questions for a survey.

21   THE BIG DEAL
Performing an experiment and determining experimental probabilities.

Cards are another common probability model. It is important that they are thoroughly shuffled for these experiments. The probability of at least one pair in a five-card hand is approximately 0.04.

22   HOW MANY MATCHES?
Performing an experiment, recording the results, and determining experimental probabilities.

Again, it is important that the students shuffle the cards thoroughly. Any cards numbered from 1 to 10 can be used. Directions for making a set are given on page 2.

23   SPIN THE QUARTER
Performing an experiment that leads to unexpected results.

This activity presents a situation in which the student's intuition will differ from reality. One would expect that heads and tails will be equally likely here, as in coin tossing. However, in coin spinning, a different physical situation is involved. A spinning coin tends to come to equilibrium and then, to fall with the heavier side down, as it slows down. For example, U.S. pennies tend to fall tails up and Canadian pennies tend to fall heads up. What did your students find for U.S. quarters? Give them time to discuss and think about their results before you explain why they occur.

24   REGULAR OR CHOCOLATE
Conducting a survey; using sampling and probability to predict the preferences of a larger group.

In this lesson the students use the class as a sample and then predict results for the entire school. Checking with the cafeteria personnel gives a direct means of learning the results for the school, and a way to check the accuracy of the prediction.

25   TV TIME
Taking a survey, finding experimental probabilities and checking to see if the probabilities apply to another sample.

Have the students work in pairs, small groups, or as a whole class for this activity. Each group can make a bar graph using the class data or the whole class can make one graph together. Each group can choose another room to survey or a pair of students can survey one other classroom and share their results with your class. Do the students think that grade-level will influence the results? Did it?

26   INSPECTING TWO DICE   *Mini-Lesson*
Listing possible outcomes, and determining probabilities of simple and compound events.

Rolling two dice leads to compound events. In listing the possible outcomes, the students must distinguish between results such as (3,4) and (4,3). Try to have the students develop their own method for completing the list, giving them as little help as possible.

There are 36 equally likely outcomes when two dice are rolled. However, when the sums of these outcomes are considered, the new list of possible events (2, 3, 4, 5, 6, 7, 8, 9, 10, 11, 12) is made up of 11 events that are *not* equally likely; for example, the expected number of occurrences of a sum of 2 is different from that of a sum of 6. Encourage discussion among the students to bring out these points.

This activity is best presented as a mini-lesson to small groups or the whole class.

27 ROLL'EM
Determining theoretical probabilities, experimenting, and comparing empirical results with theoretical results.

Each student will need a partner for this activity.

Class discussion of the comparison of the theoretical and experimental probabilities is especially appropriate here. Reemphasize that experimental probabilities result from observations made in particular experiments and may vary, while theoretical probabilities are based on fixed models and do not vary. Remind the students also that a probability tells how *likely* an event is to happen—*not* exactly how often it will happen. The combined results will support the notion that a larger number of trials will give results that more closely approach the theoretical probabilities. This concept in probability is known as the Law of Large Numbers. You may wish to review the terms *multiple* and *prime* that are used in this lesson.

28 HOW COMMON IS A "DOUBLE"?
Predicting frequencies and checking by experimenting.

This lesson involves making predictions based on previous experience with rolling 2 regular dice. The predictions and even the experimental results of individual students may vary greatly from the theoretical probability of rolling a double with two dice. However, the accumulated results of the whole class should be close to the theoretical probability of 1 double out of every 6 rolls.

29 CHECKING THE CHANCES
Performing an experiment and comparing the results with theoretical results.

In Activity 26, INSPECTING TWO DICE, the students found the theoretical probabilities of the sums that occur when two dice are tossed. This activity provides an opportunity to check the theory by experimenting.

30 A BAG OF MARBLES
Performing an experiment and comparing experimental probabilities with theoretical probabilities.

Encourage discussion of the differences between the experimental and theoretical probabilities. The students may need help with the calculations necessary to make these comparisons. The probability model in this activity, that is, drawing from a bag or container, is a very important model. It will be used again both with and without replacement.

See the note on marbles and containers in the materials section.

31 DRAWING MARBLES AND REPLACING
Performing an experiment involving drawing with replacement and comparing experimental probabilities with theoretical probabilities, both individually and in a large group.

Again, the accumulated class results should produce experimental probabilities that are closer to the theoretical probabilities than those of individual students. Class discussion should elicit comments concerning the differences between "long" and "short" run experiments. The students should be beginning to realize intuitively that as the number of experimental results increases, the closer these results should be to the theoretical model (given, of course, that the theoretical model is correct). This concept in probability is referred to as the Law of Large Numbers.

See the note on marbles and containers in the materials section.

32   CHOOSING MARBLES
Listing possible outcomes and determining probabilities.

Although this activity concerns only theoretical probabilities, experiments can be performed for each theoretical question as an extension to the lesson. Problems such as finding the Pr(red) and Pr(not red) are raised again. The concept that the sum of such complementary probabilities is one, should be emphasized in discussion. In problem 4, it is important that the students work carefully. Drawing a red and a blue marble and drawing a red and a green marble are outcomes that are twice as likely as the others. One way to demonstrate this is to assume that we can distinguish between the two red marbles and call them red_1 and red_2 when we make the list of possible outcomes: red_1, blue; red_2, blue; red_1, green; red_2, green; red_1, red_2; blue, green. Then it is easy to see that there are two ways to draw red, blue; two ways to draw red, green; and only one way to draw the other pairs. The order in which the two marbles are drawn does not matter here.

33   A LOT OF CHOICES?
Applying the multiplication principle informally.

A concise solution to this menu problem is provided by the multiplication principle; that is, the number of choices is equal to the product of the numbers of choices on each section of the menu. In the activity, the students are given the opportunity to discover this principle by listing the possible choices or combinations for meals. They should also notice the many possibilities provided by just a few choices. The multiplication principle will be stated explicitly in Activity 42.

You may wish to present this activity to groups or pairs of students in order to encourage discussion of the problems.

34   ANY MATCHES?
Predicting the results of an experiment, performing it, and comparing the experimental results with the prediction and with the theoretical probabilities.

In this activity the students compare their experimental results with their own prediction *and* the theoretical probability. Be sure that the students distinguish the two pennies in their experiment when they calculate the theoretical probability of a match. One way to do this is to write H for heads with the player's initial as a subscript; for example, write H_A for heads on Ann's penny. A discussion should follow the compilation of the class results. Again, the point that a larger number of trials usually leads to experimental results that are closer to the theoretical probability should be emphasized.

35   MOST USED LETTER
Collecting data about the frequency of events, combining data, and interpreting the results.

The students may choose whatever library books they wish to use for this experiment. The results will enable the students to make decisions as if they manufactured letters. The combined class results will improve the quality of their decisions. The six most frequently used letters in the English language are E, T, O, A, N, I according to Kerckhoff in *Cryptography* by Laurence Smith (published by W.W. Norton of New York in 1943).

36   HOW MANY WEAR GLASSES?
Using sampling and probability to predict the situation in a larger group, and checking the predictions.

This lesson provides practice in surveying a small group and using the information to predict results for a larger group. In this case, the students can go into other classes at their grade level to gather information to check their prediction.

37   DIFFERENT DICE
Listing the possible outcomes of a situation that leads to compound events; determining probabilities of events that are not equally likely.

Tossing two (octahedron) dice and adding the faces that are up leads to compound events. In listing the possible outcomes, the students must distinguish between results such as (1,8) and (8,1). There are 64 equally–likely outcomes for this situation. However, when the sums of these outcomes are considered, the new list of possible outcomes (2, 3, 4, 5, 6, 7, 8, 9, 10, 11, 12, 13, 14, 15, 16) is composed of events that are *not* equally likely. Encourage discussion among the students to emphasize these points.

38   AS THE TETRAHEDRON TUMBLES
Listing possible outcomes and determining theoretical probabilities.

The tetrahedron is somewhat limited for use as a die, because it tends not to tumble well and it lands with 1 face down and 3 faces up. However, it is a useful model to consider. The activity can be extended by performing an experiment of rolling a tetrahedron die 40 times and comparing the experimental results with the theoretical probabilities previously calculated.

39   CHOOSING PAIRS
Determining the number of pairs that can be selected from a group of people.

This activity lays groundwork for the topic of combinations. The problems are solved by listing the possible outcomes, rather than by using a formal rule.

40   THE DIE IS CAST
Determining theoretical probabilities.

This activity presents the students with "or" situations. All of the "or" situations in the lesson are *mutually exclusive;* that is, if one of the events occurs the others cannot occur. For example, rolling a "2 or a 3" with one die, is a mutually exclusive "or" situation. Consequently the solutions are found by counting the number of ways each event of the "or" situation can occur, *adding them,* and dividing by the total number of possible outcomes. For example, to find the probability of tossing a 2 or larger on a die, we count the number of ways of tossing a 2, or a 3, or a 4, or a 5, or a 6, add them, and divide by 6 (which is the total number of possible outcomes) to obtain

$$\frac{1+1+1+1+1}{6} = \frac{5}{6}.$$

You may wish to review the terms multiple and prime that are used in this lesson.

41 WHO DO YOU BELIEVE?
Predicting a probability model; experimenting to determine the appropriate model.

Bill and Vicki each claim a different probability model to be true for tossing two coins. Historically both models have been advocated. The French mathematician, D'Alembert, favored the 1/3, 1/3, 1/3 model. Experiment and theory, however, favor the 1/4, 1/4, 1/4, 1/4, model. The experiment performed by the students is usually convincing.

42 THE MULTIPLICATION PRINCIPLE *Mini-Lesson*
Introduction to using the multiplication principle to determine the number of possible outcomes of a situation.

The multiplication principle is very important in probability. It is used to calculate probabilities of repeated and compound events and to formulate the definition of independent events. Here the determination of the number of possible compound events in each situation will allow the calculation of probabilities as the next step.

This activity is best presented as a discussion lesson to a small group or the whole class and followed by Activity 43 to reinforce the new concepts. Allow the students to provide as much information as possible in the discussion, before you help them with answers.

43 USING THE MULTIPLICATION PRINCIPLE
Applying the multiplication principle to determine the number of possible outcomes and their probabilities in a situation with compound events.

You may wish to divide these problems among 4 or 5 groups of students. Have each group find out the number of possibilities for their problem using the multiplication rule, check by making a list, and share their results with the whole class.

44 FLIP AND TOSS
Listing possible outcomes and determining probabilities of compound events.

Again, we have a probability situation based on compound events; for example, a coin landing heads up *and* a die landing with 1 up. The number of possible outcomes can be found by listing or using the multiplication rule. The activity can be extended by actually performing the experiment and sharing the results with a group or the class.

45 TOOTHPASTE TOPS
Finding experimental probabilities in a situation in which there is no fixed probability model.

Here is another opportunity to compile experimental probabilities using a common object. You might want to have the students compare the results for tops of different shapes. Are they the same? Should they be combined for a class average? Or does the shape of the top make too much difference?

46 SUMMING SPINS
Determining experimental probabilities and comparing them with the theoretical probabilities for a two-spinner model.

Here the students record the results of spinning two unlike spinners and then consider the sums of these results. They calculate both the experimental and theoretical probabilities of these sums and compare them. Again, combining the experimental results of the whole class should lead to "more accurate" experimental probabilities.

Directions for making the spinners are given on page 3. Again, numbered colored cubes can be used in place of the spinners.

47   UNEVEN SPINNER
Performing an experiment and writing experimental probabilities for a situation involving events that are not equally likely; calculating the theoretical probabilities and comparing them with the experimental results.

The uneven spinner enables the teacher to determine whether the students understand the implications of equally –likely outcomes. If the students do not realize the effect of outcomes that are not equally likely, this activity should illuminate their problem. To illustrate this point, the students are asked to consider the areas of the sections of the spinner in order to calculate the theoretical probabilities.

Directions for making spinners are on page 3. The spinner for this lesson is based on 8 equal divisions with only some of the lines drawn in. If spinners are not available, the same activity can be done drawing from a bag of 1 red, 2 blue, 2 black, and 3 green color cubes.

48   HOW MANY ARE RED?
Performing an experiment and using the results in order to predict the unknown contents of a container.

In this activity, the students are presented with a sack containing an unknown number of red, yellow, and blue marbles. They are asked to predict these numbers after making 24 or 36 draws with replacement. The distinction between drawing with replacement, that is putting the marble back after each draw, and drawing without replacement, not putting the drawn marbles back, should be made clearly. Discuss how drawing without replacement would affect the experiment.

The contents for the sack are 8 red, 1 yellow, and 3 blue marbles. Any suitable container may be substituted for the sack and any objects that differ only in color may be used in place of the cubes.

49   WHAT ARE THE CHANCES OF YELLOW?
Performing an experiment and using the results in order to predict the unknown contents of a container.

Again, the students perform an experiment drawing from a sack without replacement. Reemphasize the distinction between drawing *with* and drawing *without* replacement. Any suitable container or objects may be used in place of the sack or cubes.

A discussion of how sampling might be done to check the quality of such products as light bulbs and nuts and bolts would be appropriate at this time. Consider such problems as cost of testing, how large a sample needs to be tested to be able to generalize the results, what happens when you test light bulbs for life span.

The contents of the sacks are 2 red, 4 yellow, and 6 blue marbles for the first, and 7 red, 1 yellow, and 2 blue marbles for the second.

50   CHANGING PROBABILITY
Determining probabilities for a situation involving drawing without replacement and discussing how this condition will affect the results.

The conditions of drawing with or without replacement create different probabilities for a given situation. The gumball machine provides an example of a real situation in which the students can experience the effect of drawing without replacement on the probability of obtaining a white gumball (and thus a jawbreaker). The final question suggests that the glamorous way is not always the most economical method to attain a goal.

51 HOW MUCH DOES PROBABILITY CHANGE? *Mini-Lesson*
Writing probabilities for experiments involving drawing with and without replacement; discussing the effects of these conditions on a particular experiment.

The two previous activities present experiments involving drawing with and without replacement. This activity repeats the experiment from Activity 49, drawing both with and without replacement in order to emphasize the effects of these conditions. Make a table of the combined class results and use it as a basis for discussing these effects.

This activity is best presented as a discussion lesson to small groups or the whole class. Allow the students to provide as much information as possible before you help them with the answers.

52 TREASURE CHEST
Comparing the effects of drawing with and without replacement on the probabilities for a particular situation.

Have the students work in small groups for this activity. Encourage them to discuss the problems as they work on them and continue the discussion with the whole class when each group has completed their work.

53 TREAT BY PHONE
Determining probabilities for a contest situation involving drawing with and without replacement.

Many communities promote the type of activity presented in this lesson. While students do not survey or collect data, they are asked to use data related to their own city and school. This exercise will provide students with a realistic view of their chances of winning in "contests" of this sort.

54 PENNY TOSS
Listing the possible outcomes for a game and writing the probabilities for these outcomes; discussing the fairness of the game.

The scoring for the coins represents a situation in which the outcomes are not equally likely, resulting in an unfair game. After listing the possible outcomes and calculating their probabilities, the students will be able to predict the winner of the game. Discuss how to make the game fair in small groups or with the whole class. One way to insure a fair game is to assign the points so that the probability of winning a hand multiplied by the number of points scored is equal for all players. Allow the students to develop this idea by having them test their proposed reassignments of points to see if they are fair.

55 THREE COINS ON THE TABLE
Determining the number of outcomes for a sequence of situations and determining probabilities.

The students investigate the outcomes of tossing coins. They start with just 2 and go on to 3, 4, 5, and 6. They should soon realize that listing becomes a very tedious method of determining the number of outcomes. The multiplication principle can be applied here and is much more efficient.

The extension illustrates how a probability model can be applied to real-life situations. You might want to have the students work in small groups and write up their new problems for another group to solve. One point should be stressed concerning both situations.

The probability of tossing a head or a tail or having a girl or boy remains the same—½ for each trial. Tossing five heads does not make you more likely to get a tail on the sixth toss. However, if we consider many sets of six tosses, we should find significantly more outcomes with five heads and one tail (in any order), than with six heads.

56 FOUR COINS
Performing an experiment and constructing a bar graph to illustrate the results; comparing experimental frequencies with theoretical frequencies.

Although many repetitions of this experiment are made, the results of individual students still may not yield the same number of outcomes for each event as the theory would tell you to expect. The individual bar graph will show this. A graph of the combined class results may show results that are closer to the expected. Note that this activity introduces a more formal method to calculate the expected frequencies for a given number of tosses.

57 FAMILY MEMBERS
Using sampling and probability to predict a situation for a larger group; checking the prediction.

Here is another activity that provides students the opportunity to collect data in their class and to predict the nature of a larger sample within their school. The data are easy to obtain and should prove interesting to students.

58 DICE NUMBERS
Listing outcomes and determining probabilities.

The dice numbers here yield 36 equally-likely outcomes when two dice are tossed. The students are asked to investigate the probabilities of this situation. They will need to know the terms digit, double, even number, odd number, multiple, and prime.

59 DODECAHEDRON AND ICOSAHEDRON DICE
Analyzing a probability situation; determining probabilities; experimenting and comparing experimental results with theoretical results.

This activity uses the concept of dice numbers developed in Activity 58 with dodecahedron and icosahedron dice to provide an interesting experiment. The icosahedron dice are particularly nice to use—they are close to round and tumble very well when tossed.

60 ICE CREAM
Conducting a survey; using sampling and probability to predict the preferences of a larger group.

This lesson provides practice in surveying a sample population and using the results to predict the situation for the total population. This is one of the most common applications of probability.

Students will probably discover that the results of the "forced-choice" survey (only 3 flavors to choose from) are better than the "pick any flavor you want to" survey.

61 TO THE ICE CREAM SHOPPE
Using the multiplication rule to determine probabilities.

In this lesson, the multiplication rule is applied to finding the probabilities of various combination ice cream cones.

62   WATCHING THE WEATHER
Determining probabilities; making predictions based on past observation or experimental probabilities and interpreting the results.

In this activity, the students are asked to make predictions concerning the weather based on past observations. They are asked to state what they would *expect* to happen. This is a further introduction to what is called *expectation* in probability. To determine the expectation of an event (say rain on a certain number of days), we multiply the probability of the event times the number of cases considered. The students probably have developed this concept intuitively by now.

You might want to use the extension in conjunction with a geography or science project. Note, when the weatherman says there is a 40% chance of rain, he means that in the past, given the current conditions, we can expect rain with a probability of 4/10 *provided you stay in the same location or area.*

63   A SACK OF MARBLES
Determining theoretical probabilities, performing an experiment, and comparing experimental probabilities with the theoretical probabilities.

In this activity the students will calculate the probabilities of the various orders in which 4 marbles can be drawn out of a container. If the students have difficulty calculating the theoretical probabilities, ask them to look at the list of the possible orders.

64   A GOOD MEAL
Using the multiplication rule to determine outcomes and probabilities.

Although the probabilities for this activity can be found by listing all of the 54 possible outcomes, it is much easier to use the multiplication rule. To find the total number of possible combinations, multiply the total number of soups by the total number of meats. To find the probability of a given meal, multiply the number of ways to pick the soup by the number of ways to pick the meat for that meal and divide by the total number of pairs of soups and meats—or multiply the probability of picking the soup times the probability of picking the meat. The first of these methods is the one most closely related to our original definition of probability. However, it might be interesting to show that the second method is equivalent to the first in a class discussion.

65   ROADS AND HIGHWAYS
Listing possible outcomes and determining probabilities; developing a decision-making model using a die.

The multiplication rule can be used here to determine the number of different routes that are possible. Have the students work in small groups to answer the last questions concerning the use of a tetrahedron die to choose the road routes.

66   WHAT ARE THE CHANCES?
Determining probabilities of simple and compound events.

The probability model used in this activity is a spinner with 12 numbered divisions, half of which are shaded. In the first set of questions the students must keep in mind that both of the conditions may affect the probabilities. In the second half of the lesson, they will find a set of 22 events that are not equally likely.

67 THE FIRST ACE PROBLEM
Predicting, experimenting, and comparing the experimental results to both predicted and theoretical results.

One way to find the true average for this activity is to use the following plausibility argument.

Take the 4 aces out of the deck leaving 48 cards. 1) Put one ace back. When the deck is shuffled, the ace will usually divide the deck into two parts. By symmetry, each part should, on average, be the same size, that is, 24 cards. Thus the ace would be the 25th card, and you would turn up 24 cards before finding it. 2) Add another ace. The two aces will usually divide the rest of the deck into 3 parts of 16 cards each, on the average. The first ace would be the 17th card. 3) Use 3 aces. The rest of the deck will usually be divided into 4 parts of 13 cards each, on the average. The first ace would be the 14th card. 4) With all 4 aces, the rest of the deck is divided into 5 parts. Each part would average $48 \div 5 = 9.6$ cards, so the first ace would be the 10.6th card, and you would turn up 9.6 cards on average, before finding it.

Most students will guess that the first ace will be the 13th card (dividing the 52 cards by the 4 aces). This experiment (even if accumulated for the whole class) will not usually produce results that are far enough from 13 to be very convincing. However, the students will usually accept the teacher's saying, "Yes, your experiment favored your point of view, but in the long run the results would favor 10.6."

68 FINDING THE GREEN MARBLE
Performing an experiment and then calculating the average number of trials until a specific event occurs.

In this activity the students draw from a bag of 10 marbles until they find the green one. It cannot take more than 10 draws to find it. The theoretical average is 5.5 draws.

69 HOW'S THE MARKET?
Determining experimental probabilities; predicting and interpreting the results.

This activity deals with probabilities concerning the stock market. Unless the market is reacting to some special world or U.S. trends the movement of the market should not be the same day after day. The students may discover that predicting the market is risky business at best. Discuss such questions as what observations are necessary for a 0.50 probability that stocks will go up.

70 THE THREE DICE
Performing an experiment and calculating experimental probabilities; comparing the experimental probabilities with the theoretical probabilities.

The theoretical probabilities for tossing three dice are given for this activity. The students are asked to compare their results with these values. In class discussion, see if the students can work out how the theoretical probabilities were calculated. For three dice there are $6 \times 6 \times 6$ possible outcomes for the sums from 3 to 18. Thus, to find the probability for a given sum, find the number of ways it can occur and divide by 216.

71 GAME OF DIGITS
Recording the results from a game, calculating the theoretical probability of winning, and reassigning points to make the game fair.

To determine the theoretical probabilities for their game, the students must calculate the number of possible outcomes and the number of ways each player can win. Since there are 3 choices for each of 3 players, there are $3 \times 3 \times 3$ possible outcomes for a given round of play. Player A can win with outcomes 111, 222, or 333 only. Player C can win with outcomes 123, 132, 213, 231, 321, or 312 only. This leaves 18 ways out of 27 for player B to win! How many points should players A and C be assigned for each round they win in order to make the game fair? Have the students try out their suggestions to see if they are really fair. The number of points to assign can be determined by using the least common multiple of the numbers of ways the players can win. Player A can win in 3 ways, player B in 18 ways and player C in 6 ways. The LCM is 18. For a fair game, the product of the number of ways the player can win and the number of points won should equal the LCM. Thus, for this game player A would receive 6 points for each win; player B, 1 point for each win; and player C 3 points for each win. Did any of the students work out this point system on their own?

72 NAME THE CONTAINER
Performing an experiment and using the results to predict the contents of a container; discussing the effect of varying the number of trials and drawing with and without replacement.

The students know the total number of objects in the containers, but not the ratio of the two colors. They are asked to predict this ratio after experimenting. In discussion, emphasize the effects of drawing with and without replacement.

Marble Distributions:

	A	B	C	D	E		A	B	C	D	E
Red	25	20	15	10	5	Red	15	5	20	25	10
Blue	5	10	15	20	25	Blue	15	25	10	5	20

Ask the students to make up their own rules for the marble distribution if they want to repeat the experiment.

73 A WORLD RECORD
Performing an experiment, and using theoretical probability to analyze potential outcomes.

This is an interesting experiment. While long runs without doubles might occur, the probability associated with the experiment suggests such long runs to be unusual events. The students have an opportunity to apply their knowledge of probability to explain why the number of rolls without producing doubles is generally limited.

HEADS OR TAILS?

Look at a penny. One side is called "heads".

Australian   U.S.   Canadian

One side is called "tails".

Australian   U.S.   Canadian

When you toss your penny, it will land on one side or the other—*heads or tails.*
(It *might* land on its edge, but then it will fall over to one side or the other.)
1. If you tossed a coin 50 times, how many heads would you expect? _____

TRY IT! Keep a list for 50 tosses.
2. Write H for heads and T for tails.
Record the number of heads and tails in
the table.
3. How many heads did you get? _____
4. Are you surprised at the results? _____
Why or why not? _____

RESULT	NUMBER
Heads	
TOTAL	50

Extension. Combine your results with a group or the whole class.
How many tosses altogether in your group? _____
How many heads? _____
Are you surprised? _____
Why or why not? _____

MATERIALS: penny, pencil.

YELLOW-RED-GREEN

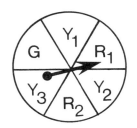

GAME I
To play this game, you need a spinner like the one on the left and a partner. The object of the game is to guess the outcome of each spin.

First guess the color the spinner arrow will stop on and then flip the spinner. The possible guesses for this game are: Yellow, Red, Green. (You do not need to pay attention to the numbers that go with the colors for this game.)
1. Play the game 25 times each, taking turns. Record your guesses in a table like the one below.

	Player A Result	Points	Guess	Player B Result	Points
1					
2					
3					

2. If you have developed a technique for guessing, write it here.

GAME II
This game is played like Game I, with one exception: When you guess this time, you must guess both the color, and the number.
The possible guesses are: Green, $Yellow_1$, Red_1, $Yellow_2$, Red_2, $Yellow_3$.
3. Play the game 25 times each, taking turns. Record your results in a table like the one for Game I above.
4. Was it easier or more difficult to win points in this game? _____
Explain your answer. _____
5. How is this game different from Game I? _____
6. Is there any way to "outguess" the spinner for Game II? _____
If not, what rule or game changes would you make so this is not a pure guessing game?

MATERIALS: spinner*, partner, pencil, paper.

*This activity can also be done by guessing the outcome of drawing a color cube or counter from a bag instead of using the spinner. You will need 1 green, 2 red, and 3 yellow cubes. Label the red cubes 1 and 2; and the yellow 1, 2, and 3. To play the games guess what cube you will draw, draw, record your guess and the result, return the cube to the bag, mix the cubes, and start over.

SPIN A COLOR

To do this activity, you will need a spinner like the one in the picture.

Suppose this spinner is spun 27 times.
1. How many times would you *expect* the spinner to stop on yellow? _____
2. How many times on red? _____
3. How many times on blue? _____
4. TRY THE EXPERIMENT. KEEP A TALLY. Put the results in the table below.

	EXPECTED RESULTS	ACTUAL RESULTS	
		TALLY	NUMBER
Yellow			
Blue			
Red			
TOTAL	27		27

5. Find the difference between your experimental results and what you expected:
      a) Yellow: _____
      b) Blue: _____
      c) Red: _____
6. Are you surprised at the results? _____ Why or why not? _____

MATERIALS: spinner*, pencil.

*This activity can also be done by using a bag or other container and 3 color cubes (1 yellow, 1 blue, 1 red) in place of the spinner. Draw a cube from the bag instead of spinning. Put it back and shake the bag thoroughly before the next draw.

THINKING ABOUT MORE SPINNERS

Tell what you think will happen on 100 spins of each of the spinners below.

1.

COLOR	EXPECTED
Blue (B)	
Yellow (Y)	
Green (G)	
Red (R)	
TOTAL	100

2.

NUMBER	EXPECTED
1	
2	
3	
4	
5	
TOTAL	100

3.

NUMBER	EXPECTED
1	
2	
3	
4	
5	
6	
7	
8	
9	
10	
TOTAL	100

Extension. Get the spinners and do the experiments.
Compare your results with what you expected.

MATERIALS: pencil, spinners (optional).

GUESSING THE COLORS

"I have a blue, a red, and a yellow card. I put them on the table in a row. Can you guess the order?"

"Wow—that's hard. I could *never* do that!"

1. How hard is it? _____
2. How many orders are there? (Guess.) _____

Here is one order:
Blue   Red   Yellow

3. List all of the orders. Use cards to help you.

Blue	Red	Yellow

4. How many orders are there? _____
5. How many *wrong* ways could Bill guess? _____
6. How many *right* ways could Bill guess? _____

MATERIALS: cards (8 red, 8 blue, 8 yellow), pencil.

HOW'S YOUR POP?

Suppose three cups of cola drink are on the table. One is Coke, one is Pepsi, and one is RC Cola. The cups have labels A, B, and C only. You are to taste from each cup and tell which cup contains which cola.

1. Make a list of all of the possible ways the colas could have been put into the three cups.

__A__	__B__	__C__
Coke	Pepsi	RC Cola
_____	_____	_____
_____	_____	_____
_____	_____	_____
_____	_____	_____
_____	_____	_____

2. If you guessed *without* tasting, you would have 1 out of _____ chances of being correct.
3. If 24 students guessed without tasting, how many would you expect to guess all three colas correctly? _____
4. If all of the students in your class guessed without tasting, how many would you expect to guess all three colas correctly? _____

TRY THE EXPERIMENT WITH YOUR CLASS.
Ask your teacher to prepare 3 identical cups labeled A, B, and C: one with Coke, one with Pepsi, and one with RC Cola for each student.
Taste a small amount of cola from each cup.
5. Write down which cola comes from which bottle. According to your taste,
   A is _____, B is _____, and C is _____.
6. How many students in your class got all three colas right? _____
7. Is this more or less than you expected if they were just guessing? _____
8. Do you think that the results in your class are good enough to say that your class can tell the colas apart by tasting? _____
Why or why not? _____

MATERIALS: paper cups (3 for each student), colas (Coke, Pepsi, RC)*, pencil.
   *This activity can also be done using 3 varieties of chewing gum in place of the colas.

ROLLING A DIE

This is a die.
Two of them are called dice.

When you play COOTIE, you roll one die.
When you play MONOPOLY, you roll two dice.
When you play YAHTZEE, you roll five dice.

A die may show any of these on its top face:

1   2   3   4   5   6

1. Roll a die 60 times. Keep a tally of how many 1's, 2's, 3's, 4's, 5's and 6's you get.

NUMBER OF DOTS	TALLY	NUMBER
1		
2		
3		
4		
5		
6		
TOTAL		

2. Do the results surprise you? _____
Why or why not? _____

MATERIALS: one die, pencil.

ROLLING THE DODECAHEDRON

Not all dice are cubes.
A dodecahedron has 12 faces, each with 5 edges.
You will need a dodecahedron die with faces
numbered 1 to 12.

1. Roll it 120 times. Keep a tally of the number of times each number
comes up.

NUMBER	TALLY	NUMBER OF TIMES
1		
2		
3		
4		
5		
6		
7		
8		
9		
10		
11		
12		
TOTAL		120

2. Are you surprised at your results?
Why or why not? _____

MATERIALS: one dodecahedron die, pencil.

PROBABILITY

When you toss a coin, it will land either heads or tails. You can't be sure which will happen.

If you throw a regular die, it can land showing a 1, or a 2, or a 3, or a 4, or a 5, or a 6. You can't be sure which will happen. When this spinner is spun, you can't be sure what color you'll get.

In these situations and others like them, you are dealing with *probability*. When you toss a coin, most people will say that the *probability of getting a head* is 1/2.
Why do you think they say this?
There are two ways the coin can land—heads or tails. Each way is just as likely as the other. Only one way is a head.
So we say
 the probability of a head (when tossing a coin) is:

$$\frac{\text{the number of ways to get a head}}{\text{the number of ways a coin can land}} = \frac{1}{2}.$$

1. What is the probability of a *tail* when you toss a coin? _____
Hint. How many ways can you get a tail? How many ways can the coin land?
2. What is the probability of a *red* when you spin the spinner above? _____
Hint. How many ways can you get a red? How many colors are there?
3. What is the probability of a *5* when you toss a die? _____
Hint. How many ways can you get a 5? How many ways can a die land?

MATERIALS: coins, spinners, dice, pencil.

FINDING PROBABILITIES

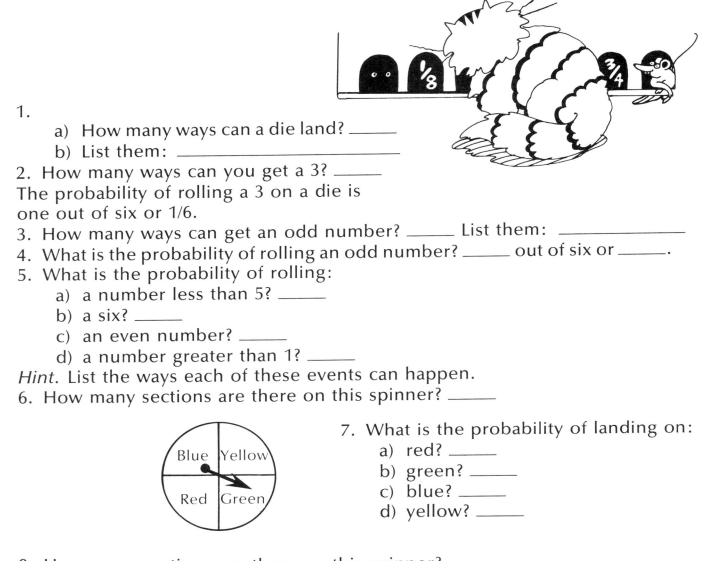

1.
   a) How many ways can a die land? _____
   b) List them: _____
2. How many ways can you get a 3? _____
The probability of rolling a 3 on a die is
one out of six or 1/6.
3. How many ways can get an odd number? _____ List them: _____
4. What is the probability of rolling an odd number? _____ out of six or _____.
5. What is the probability of rolling:
   a) a number less than 5? _____
   b) a six? _____
   c) an even number? _____
   d) a number greater than 1? _____
Hint. List the ways each of these events can happen.
6. How many sections are there on this spinner? _____

7. What is the probability of landing on:
   a) red? _____
   b) green? _____
   c) blue? _____
   d) yellow? _____

8. How many sections are there on this spinner? _____
9. What is the probability of landing on:
   a) red? _____
   b) green? _____
   c) blue? _____
   d) yellow? _____

10. What makes problem 9 different from problems 5 and 7?

MATERIALS: pencil, one die (optional), spinners (optional).

SHORTCUTS FOR WRITING PROBABILITIES

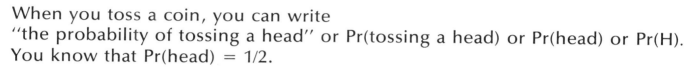

You know that if you roll a regular die,
the probability of rolling a 4 is 1/6.
Another way of writing this is:

Pr(rolling a 4 with a die) = 1/6.

If we *know* we are talking about a die,
this can be shortened to:

Pr(4) = 1/6.

When you toss a coin, you can write
"the probability of tossing a head" or Pr(tossing a head) or Pr(head) or Pr(H).
You know that Pr(head) = 1/2.

Write a shorter form for the following probabilities:
1. The probability of a tail when tossing a coin _____
2. The probability of spinning "blue" on this
red, blue, and yellow spinner _____
_____

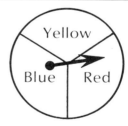

3. The probability of an even number when you roll a die _____
4. The probability of drawing an ace from a deck of 52 cards _____
Write these probabilities in words:
5. Pr(T) = 1/2 _____
6. Pr(3 on a die) = 1/6 _____
7. Pr(yellow or blue on the spinner above) = 1/3 + 1/3 _____
_____
8. Pr(making a hit in a baseball game) = .300 _____
_____
9. Pr(rain) = 40% _____

MATERIALS: pencil.

ARE YOU CERTAIN? OR ARE YOU IMPOSSIBLE?

Some things are *certain* to happen. If today is Friday, you can be certain the next day is Saturday.
Some other things are *impossible*. It is impossible to spin a purple with this spinner.

Some other things may or may not happen. It may rain, or it may not. Things that may or may not happen are *possible*.
Let's decide which of the following are certain (C), possible (P), and impossible (I).

1. You walk down the block and pass a live dinosaur. _____
2. You throw a 6 on a die. _____
3. You get a head when you toss a coin. _____
4. Your teacher is over 16 years old. _____
5. You will ride on a jet airplane before the end of the year. _____
6. The moon will be proven to be made out of green cheese. _____
7. You will be given a homework assignment in mathematics this year. _____
8. Your school has a principal. _____
9. You will go to Disneyland sometime. _____
10. You will learn to play the flute. _____
11. Can you think of other events that are certain? Possible? Impossible? Write your own list. Use the same code letters.
12. What do you think the probability of an impossible event will be? _____
Hint. How many ways can an impossible event happen?
We say that the *probability of an impossible event is zero*, because it never happens.
13. What do you think the probability of a certain event will be? _____
We say that the *probability of a certain event is one*, because it always happens.

MATERIALS: pencil.

SOME PROBABILITIES

Fill in the probabilities for the spinner:

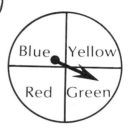

1. a) Pr(blue) = _____
   b) Pr(red) = _____
   c) Pr(not red) = _____
       (*Hint*. List and count the ways you can land on a color that is not red.)
   d) Pr(yellow or green) = _____
   e) Pr(a color) = _____   [This is certain.]
   f) Pr(brown) = _____   [This is impossible.]

2. Fill in the probabilities for a die:
   a) Pr(2) = _____
   b) Pr(odd number) = _____
   c) Pr(9) = _____ [Impossible]
   d) Pr(number less than 7) = _____ [Certain]
   e) Pr(4) = _____
   f) Pr(not 4) = _____
   (*Hint*. List and count the ways a die can land with 4 not showing.)
   g) Pr(4) + Pr(not 4) = _____

Try these problems.
3. On a die, what is: Pr(1) + Pr(2) + Pr(3) + Pr(4) + Pr(5) + Pr(6)?
4. When the probability of something happening is 1, that something is (certain, impossible). _____
5. If something is impossible, what is its probability? _____

Bonus.
6. On a spinner, Pr(green) = 1/3. What is Pr(not green)? _____
7. If the probability of not winning a game is 5/7, what is the probability of winning the game if ties are not allowed? _____

MATERIALS: pencil, spinners (optional), one die (optional).

SOME PROBABILITY RULES

Some Probability Rules

1. *If something is impossible, the probability of its happening is 0.* Give some examples of impossible events.

2. *If something is certain to happen, the probability it will happen is 1.* Give some examples of certain events.

3. *Most things are neither certain nor impossible. Most probabilities are between 0 and 1.*

4. *A probability can be written as a fraction, a decimal, or a per cent.*
What is the probability of getting a 2 on a die? _____
We can write it as
$$Pr(2) = 1/6.$$
What is the probability of getting a tail on a coin?
We can write it as
$$Pr(tail) = 1/2 \text{ or } 0.5 \text{ or } 50\%.$$

5. *The probability something will happen plus the probability it will* not *happen is 1.*
What can happen when you roll a die? Let's make a list:
1, _____, _____, _____, _____, _____, _____.
What is the probability of rolling a 3? Let's figure it out.
How many ways can you get a 3? (1)
How many things can happen altogether? (6)
So
$$Pr(3) = 1/6.$$
What is the probability of not getting a 3? How many ways can you not get a 3? (5)
So
$$Pr(not\ 3) = 5/6;$$
and
$$Pr(3) + Pr(not\ 3) = 1/6 + 5/6 = 1.$$

MATERIALS: pencil.

PROBABILITY OF NOT GETTING SOMETHING

1. For each probability given, write the probability of that event *not* happening.

Hint. What is Pr(something happens) + Pr(it doesn't happen)?

	Probability It Happens	Probability It Doesn't Happen
a)	3/4	_____
b)	1/2	_____
c)	1/9	_____
d)	0.6	_____
e)	0.54	_____
f)	7/8	_____
g)	0.1	_____
h)	0	_____

Something either happens or it doesn't.

Right on!

2. Fill in the blanks.

	Probability It Happens	Probability It Doesn't Happen
a)	2/3	_____
b)	0.9	_____
c)	_____	0.3
d)	_____	3/5
e)	_____	0
f)	2/9	_____
g)	_____	1/2
h)	_____	0.56
i)	0.12	_____

3. What is the secret to figuring out these problems? _____

_____

MATERIALS: pencil.

SOME SPORTS QUESTIONS

Use the past records given in each problem to calculate the probabilities.

1. A basketball player has made 74% of her free throws. What per cent has she missed? _____

2. A baseball player has a batting average of .347. If this represents the probability he will get a hit, what is the chance he will *not* get a hit? _____

3. A tennis player has won 2/3 of her matches. Based on her previous record, what is the probability she will *lose* a match? _____

4. In the past 10 races, RACING PACER, the famous thoroughbred, has won 8. What is the probability, based on this, that RACING PACER will *win* his next race? _____

5. Ron Speedy, the baseball player, has tried to steal second base 29 times this season. He has been successful 17 times. Do you think his chances of stealing second base the next time he tries are good or bad? _____ Why? _____

6. George has jumped over 5.5 m in the long jump in 6 out of 12 track meets this year. What is the probability he will jump *under* 5.5 m in the next meet? _____

7. The school basketball team has won 3 out of 5 games this season. Based on this record, what is the probability they will *lose* the next game? _____

8. Susan has broken 65 seconds for the 100 meter free style in swimming in 75% of her races. What is the probability that she will *not* break 65 seconds at her next meet? _____

MATERIALS: pencil

SPIN A NUMBER

You will need a spinner like the one below for this experiment.

1. In 100 spins, how many times would you expect each number to come up? _____ Why? _____

2. Spin the spinner 100 times. Keep a tally. Record the results in the table below.

NUMBER	TALLY	TOTAL
1		
2		
3		
4		
5		
6		
7		
8		
9		
10		
TOTAL		100

3. Are your results the same as what you expected? _____
How do you explain this? _____

MATERIALS: spinner*, pencil.

*This activity can also be done by drawing cubes labeled 1 to 10 from a bag instead of using the spinner.

COUNTING WORD LENGTH

Cut out a newspaper article.
Use one that is fairly long.

1. Keep a tally of the length of the words.

1 letter	_____	6 letters	_____
2 letters	_____	7 letters	_____
3 letters	_____	8 letters	_____
4 letters	_____	9 letters	_____
5 letters	_____	10 letters	_____

more than 10 letters _____

2. How many words were there altogether? _____
3. Which word length occured most often? _____
4. Write the fraction of *your* news column that has each word length.

1 letter	_____	6 letters	_____
2 letters	_____	7 letters	_____
3 letters	_____	8 letters	_____
4 letters	_____	9 letters	_____
5 letters	_____	10 letters	_____

more than 10 letters _____

These are the probabilities for word lengths *based on your column. They are called experimental* or *empirical probabilities.* (Experimental means the same as empirical.)
5. Do you think they will be the same for another column? _____
6. TRY IT. (Use the back of this sheet for your tally.)
7. Which word length occurs most often this time? _____
Is it the same as before? _____ Why do you think this is so? _____

Extension. Combine your results with a group or the whole class.
Which word length is most frequent? _____ Is it the same as yours? _____
What word length do you think is most common in English? _____
Why? _____

MATERIALS: newspaper, pencil.

FINDING PROBABILITIES FROM EXPERIMENTS

Sometimes you can't figure out or even guess what a probability will be until you do an experiment. For example, suppose you toss a thumbtack. There are two ways it can land:

Point Down   Point Up

There is no reason to suspect that the probability of "Point Up" is the same as the probability of "Point Down". In fact, for most thumbtacks, it isn't.

EXPERIMENT

1. Put 10 identical thumbtacks into a paper cup.
Shake the cup and turn it face down on your desk.
Count the number of thumbtacks landing point up.
Do the experiment 20 times. Record your results on another paper.

What is the total number of tosses you have made? _____

2. What is your experimental probability of a thumbtack landing point up? _____

3. Express this figure as a two-place decimal. _____

4. Combine your results with those of other class members. Find the average probability of a tack landing point up for the whole class. _____

Extension. How do you think your results would be affected if the point of the tack were very long, for example, 1 meter long? If it were very short, for example, 1 millimeter long?

MATERIALS: paper cup, 10 identical thumbtacks, pencil, paper.

CARS, CARS, CARS

Suppose you want to be able to predict the colors or types of cars that pass your school. Here is one way to try.

Several teams of two, an observer and recorder, will be needed to collect data.

I. THIS WEEK
Choose a place (in front of the school or on a particular street corner) and record data about 100 cars that pass by your station. Each team should collect data from one category, color or type of car.
The observer will call out the data, and the recorder will tally and note when 100 observations are made.
Collect data in these categories:

COLOR			TYPE	
Blue	Black	Yellow	Sedan	Pick-Up Truck
Red	White	Other	Sports Car	Camper
	Green		Station Wagon	Van

Use the data collected to write *experimental probabilities* that these events will occur at the same time next week.

1. <u>COLOR</u>

Pr(Blue) = _____   Pr(Red) = _____
Pr(Black) = _____   Pr(White) = _____   Pr(Other) = _____

2. <u>TYPE</u>

Pr(Sedan) = _____   Pr(Station Wagon) = _____
Pr(Sports Car) = _____   Pr(Pick-Up Truck) = _____
Pr(Van) = _____   Pr(Camper) = _____   Pr(Other) = _____

II. SAME TIME NEXT WEEK
Return to your station and record data for 100 more cars.
3. Calculate the experimental probabilities for your observations.
4. How do these compare with last week's experimental probabilities? _____
5. Can you give any reasons why the results might not be close? _____
6. Do you think that it was important that you collected the data at the same time both weeks? _____

Extension. Write about your experience.

MATERIALS: pencil, paper.

THE BIG DEAL

An ordinary playing card deck has 52 cards.
There are 4 suits: clubs ♣ , diamonds ♦ ,
hearts ♥ and spades ♠ . There are 13 cards
in each suit: Ace, 2, 3, 4, 5, 6, 7, 8, 9, 10, Jack,
Queen, and King.

Take a deck of cards. Shuffle the cards thoroughly. Deal out 10 hands of
5 cards each. (You will have 2 cards left).

1. How many times did you get a pair in one of the hands of 5 cards? _____
A pair is two cards with the same number. Try this 5 times (for a total of
50 hands). Keep track of the number of hands that contain pairs.

2. How many hands had a pair this time? _____

3. What fraction of your hands contained a pair? _____
This is your experimental probability.

4. Write this fraction as a two-place decimal. _____

5. Would you always get this fraction in 50 hands? _____

6. Did your friends? _____

MATERIALS: playing cards, pencil.

HOW MANY MATCHES?

You will need 10 cards numbered from 1 to 10. Write the numbers from 1 to 10 on a piece of paper. Turn your number cards face down and shuffle them thoroughly. Turn them over one by one. Record the number on the first card you turn up beside the 1 on your paper, the second card beside the 2, and so on.

1. Did you get any matches? (A match occurs when the number on the paper matches the number on the card.) _____

2. Do this experiment 10 times. Record the number of matches each time in the table below.

TIME	NUMBER OF MATCHES
1	
2	
3	
4	
5	
6	
7	
8	
9	
10	
TOTAL	

There were 100 possible chances for a match.
3. How many matches did you get? _____
4. According to your results, what is the experimental probability of a match? _____
5. Express this probability as a two-place decimal. _____

MATERIALS: 10 cards (numbered 1 to 10), pencil, paper.

SPIN THE QUARTER

A new quarter will work best.

Get a quarter. Spin it by standing it on edge, holding it with the forefinger of one hand and snapping it with the forefinger of the other hand. Make sure that the coin is on a level surface where it is able to spin freely without hitting anything.

1. How many heads would you expect to occur in 50 spins? _____

2. Spin your quarter 50 times and keep a tally of how many heads and tails you get. Record your results in the table below.

RESULT	TALLY	NUMBER
Heads		
Tails		
TOTAL		50

3. Do your results agree with what you expected? _____

4. How do you explain this? _____

Extension. Try this experiment with a Canadian penny and an American penny. What happens? _____
Are you surprised? _____

MATERIALS: quarter, pencil.

REGULAR OR CHOCOLATE?

For your class, find out:

1. How many students drink chocolate milk for lunch. _____

2. How many students drink regular milk for lunch. _____

3. The experimental probability that a student in your class will drink chocolate milk for lunch is: _____

4. Do you think this experimental probability would be accurate for the whole school? _____
Why? _____

5. If so, how many students would you expect to drink chocolate milk in your school? _____

Now, go to the school lunch people. Find out:

6. How many chocolate milks were sold at lunch today. _____

7. How many regular milks were sold at lunch today. _____

8. What is the experimental probability that a student in the school will drink chocolate milk for lunch? _____

9. How close were your answers to questions 3 and 6? Were the results in your class pretty much like the results for the school? _____

Extension. Choose another food that has different varieties such as ice cream or sandwiches and do the same experiment.

MATERIALS: pencil, paper.

TV TIME

1. Make a list of 10 TV shows that you think your classmates like.

2. Take a survey in your class. Ask the students to choose their favorite show from the list.

3. Make a bar graph from the results.
To do this you will need a large piece of graph paper with big squares. Draw a horizontal base line about three squares from the bottom of the graph paper. Write the names of the TV shows under this line and have each student put his or her name in a square above his or her favorite show.

4. Which show is the most popular with members of your class? _____

5. What is the experimental probability that a student in your class likes that show best? _____

6. What are the experimental probabilities for the other shows?

7. Use your experimental probabilities to predict the favorites in another class. Have two or three students take a survey of another class. How do your predictions compare with the actual results? _____

8. Do you think the grade-level of the class you chose would affect the results? _____
Why or why not? _____

MATERIALS: paper, graph paper, pencil, TV guide (optional).

INSPECTING TWO DICE

Take a red die and a white die (or any two dice of different colors). If you roll them, there are many ways they could land. Three and five can appear in 2 ways:

red die   white die   red die   white die

1. List all the possible ways that 2 dice can land on another sheet of paper. Your list should look like the one started below.

1,1	2,1	3,1	4,1	5,1	6,1
1,2	—	—	—	—	—
1,3	—	—	—	—	—
1,4	—	—	—	—	—
1,5	—	—	—	—	—
1,6	—	—	—	—	6,6

2. How many ways are there for the red die to land? _____
3. How many ways are there for the white die to land? _____
4. How many ways are there for the two dice to land? _____

Now suppose you count or add the dots on both dice when you roll them. Use your list to answer the following questions.

5. What is the smallest sum you can roll? _____ The largest? _____
6. Is it possible to roll all of the numbers in between? _____
7. List all of the possible sums: _____
8. Can you roll some of the sums in more than one way? _____
9. Give an example: _____
10. a) How many ways can you roll a sum of 12? _____ List them: _____
    b) Of 11? _____ List them: _____
    c) Of 1? _____ List them: _____
    d) Of 8? _____ List them: _____
11. Which sum has the most ways to occur? _____
12. Find the following probabilities for the *sums* from rolling 2 dice:

    a) Pr(12) = _____   d) Pr(2,3, or 12) = _____
    b) Pr(6) = _____   e) Pr(7 or 11) = _____
    c) Pr(7) = _____   f) Pr(number greater than 8) = _____

MATERIALS: pencil, 2 dice of different colors (optional).

ROLL 'EM

Choose a partner and each take a colored die. One of you use red and the other green or white. Roll your dice and find the sum of the spots on the two dice.

1. How many pairs of numbers are possible when the two dice are rolled? _____
Remember 2 on the red die and 4 on the white is different from 4 on the red and 2 on the white.

2. List the pairs that add to 7: _____

3. What is the Pr(sum of 7)? _____

4. Write the following probabilities:

a) Pr(sum of 12) = _____   d) Pr(2 fives) = _____

b) Pr(sum of 8) = _____   e) Pr(a five and a three) = _____

c) Pr(sum of 4) = _____   f) Pr(a difference of 3) = _____

Hint. Use your list of possible results from Activity 26 or make a list of the pairs that add to the number.

5. Now try this experiment. Roll your dice 36 times and keep a tally of the sum of each roll.

SUM	TALLY	NUMBER	SUM	TALLY	NUMBER
2			7		
3			8		
4			9		
5			10		
6			11		
			12		

6. a) How many sums of 7 did you get? _____ b) Of 12? _____
c) Of 4? _____ d) Of 9? _____

7. a) From your experiment what is your *experimental probability* of:
a sum of 7? _____ b) Of 12? _____ c) Of 4? _____ d) Of 9? _____

8. How do these results compare with the theoretical probabilities? _____

Extension. Combine your results with a group or the whole class. How do your combined experimental probabilities compare with the theoretical probabilities? _____

Are they closer than for individual pairs? _____

Why do you think this is so? _____

MATERIALS: 2 dice of different colors, pencil.

HOW COMMON IS A "DOUBLE"?

In Monopoly, you get an extra turn when you throw a "double" with the 2 dice. (A "double" means both dice show the same number.)

GUESS

1. You would expect one double out of every _____ rolls of two dice?

2. How many doubles would you expect in 100 rolls of 2 dice? _____

EXPERIMENT
Roll two dice 100 times and keep a tally of the doubles.

3. How many doubles did you get in 100 rolls? _____

4. *Based on the experiment,* you might expect to get one double out of every _____ rolls, on the average.

MATERIALS: 2 dice, pencil.

CHECKING THE CHANCES

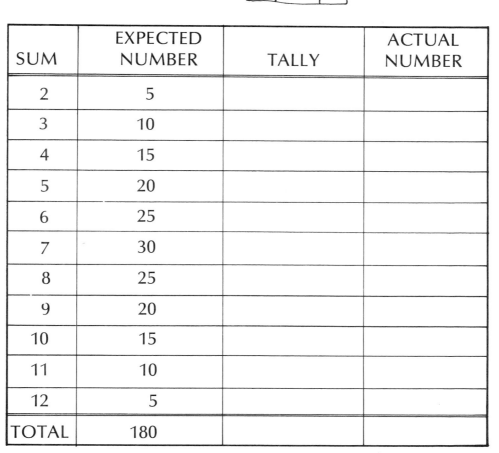

177 178 179 180

1. Throw two dice 180 times. Record the results in the table below. Notice that the second column gives the expected results based on theoretical probability.

SUM	EXPECTED NUMBER	TALLY	ACTUAL NUMBER
2	5		
3	10		
4	15		
5	20		
6	25		
7	30		
8	25		
9	20		
10	15		
11	10		
12	5		
TOTAL	180		

2. How do you explain the differences between the expected and actual numbers above? _____

3. Were the results close enough to satisfy you? _____
Why or why not?_____

Bonus. Explain where the expected numbers came from.

MATERIALS: 2 dice, pencil.

A BAG OF MARBLES

Put 10 marbles (3 blue, 4 green, 2 red, 1 yellow) into a paper bag. Suppose you shake the bag and take out a marble without looking.

1. What is:
   a) Pr(blue) ? _____
   b) Pr(green) ? _____
   c) Pr(red) ? _____
   d) Pr(yellow) ? _____
2. Try this experiment 50 times. Keep a tally of the colors you draw. Remember to put your marble back after each draw and shake the bag.

COLOR	TALLY	NUMBER OF TIMES DRAWN	FRACTION OF TIMES DRAWN
Blue			
Green			
Red			
Yellow			
TOTAL		50	

3. How do your experimental results compare with the theoretical probabilities? (*Hint.* Change the theoretical probabilities to fiftieths.) Are they the same? _____ A little different? _____ A lot different? _____ Why do you think this happened? _____

_____

MATERIALS: pencil, marbles (3 blue, 4 green, 2 red, 1 yellow), paper bag.

DRAWING MARBLES AND REPLACING

Place 20 marbles in a container (10 red,
6 yellow, 4 blue).
1. Remove a marble, and record the color.
Replace the marble and shake the container.
Try the experiment 10 times.

Mix the marbles
after each draw!

COLOR	TALLY	NUMBER
Red		
Yellow		
Blue		
TOTAL		10

2. Write your experimental probability for red: _____
3. Write the theoretical probability: Pr(red) = _____
Place the results of your whole class on the chalkboard.
4. Find the *experimental probability* of drawing a red marble for the
class. _____
5. Is this *experimental probability* closer to the theoretical probability than
yours was? _____

Experimental probabilities depend on a large number of trials in order to be
valuable to use.

MATERIALS: container, marbles (10 red, 6 yellow, 4 blue), pencil.

CHOOSING MARBLES

For each problem below, after a marble is drawn from the bag and recorded, it is replaced and the marbles are mixed before the next draw.

A bag contains 1 red marble, 1 blue marble, and 1 green marble.

1. If you choose 1 marble at a time, what is:
   a) Pr(choosing a red) = _____
   b) Pr(choosing a blue) = _____
   c) Pr(not choosing a red) = _____

2. Suppose 2 marbles are drawn at a time, from a new bag. List the pairs that can be drawn:
   <u>blue</u>, <u>green</u>;_____

3. How many pairs are possible? _____

4. Find:
   a) Pr(drawing blue and green) = _____
   b) Pr(not drawing a red) = _____
   c) Pr(drawing red and green) = _____

A bag contains 4 marbles: 2 red, 1 blue, 1 green.

5. If you draw 1 marble at a time, what is:
   a) Pr(choosing a blue) = _____
   b) Pr(choosing a red) = _____
   c) Pr(not choosing a red) = _____

6. Suppose two marbles are drawn at a time from the new bag. List the pairs that can be drawn: <u>blue</u>, <u>green</u>; _____
   Pretend you can tell the 2 red marbles apart.

7. Find:
   a) Pr(blue and green) = _____
   b) Pr(2 reds) = _____
   c) Pr(red and blue) = _____

Extension. Try each of the experiments 48 times. Keep a tally of your results and compare them to the theoretical probabilities you calculated above.

MATERIALS: pencil, paper bag and marbles (optional).

A LOT OF CHOICES?

Sometimes it's hard to choose meals
from a menu. There are so many things to eat!

1. If there is one choice of soup(S), main dish (M), and dessert (D), how
many different complete meals are available? _____
2. How many complete meals would you have to choose from if there are
1 soup, 2 main dishes, and 1 dessert? _____
3. List the possible meals for: 2 soups (tomato, onion); 2 main dishes
(steak, chicken); 2 desserts (pudding, cake).

SOUP	MAIN DISH	DESSERT
_____	_____	_____
_____	_____	_____
_____	_____	_____
_____	_____	_____
_____	_____	_____
_____	_____	_____
_____	_____	_____
_____	_____	

4. How many meals could be chosen from a menu having:
    a) 2 soups, 3 main dishes, 4 desserts? _____
    b) 2 soups, 6 main dishes, 5 desserts? _____
Hint. Make up your own soups, main dishes, and desserts, and list the
possible meals.
5. Are you surprised at the results? _____
6. Can you suggest a shorter way than making lists to solve these problems?

MATERIALS: pencil, paper.

ANY MATCHES

Choose a partner and each get a penny.
You are going to toss your pennies and
record if they match—heads and heads or
tails and tails.

1. If you did this experiment 50 times, how
many matches would you predict? _____

2. What fraction of the time would you expect
matches? _____

3. Do the experiment 50 times and tally the
results.

RESULTS	TALLY	NUMBER
Matches		
No Matches		
TOTAL		50

4. What fraction of the time did you get a match? _____
This is the *experimental probability*.

5. Is it close to what you predicted? _____

6. List the ways your two coins could land. Distinguish between your penny
and your friend's. _____

7. Use your list to find
Pr(matching coins) = _____

8. How does your *experimental probability* compare with this *theoretical
probability*? _____

Extension. Combine your results with a group or the whole class.

How do your combined results compare with the theoretical probability?
Is the class experimental probability closer to the theoretical than yours was?
How do you explain this?

MATERIALS: 2 pennies, a partner, pencil.

MOST USED LETTER

In this activity, we want to try to find the most frequently used letters from the alphabet.

1. Choose a library book and open to any page you wish. Count the first 100 words. Tally the number of times each letter is used in those 100 words.

A	G	M	T
B	H	N	U
C	I	O	V
D	J	P	W
E	K	Q	X
F	L	R	Y
		S	Z

2. Which letter was used most? _____
3. Do you think this is the letter in the alphabet that is used most often? _____
4. Combine your results with a group or the whole class.
   a) What letter did your classmates find was used most often? _____
   b) If you were buying letters for signs, which letter would you buy most of? _____
   c) Which letter would you buy fewest of? _____

MATERIALS: library book, pencil.

HOW MANY WEAR GLASSES?

1. How many students are there in your room? _____

2. How many students in your room wear glasses? _____

3. What is the experimental probability a student in your room wears glasses? _____

Answer the following questions:

4. How many students are in your grade in your school? _____

5. How many students in your grade would you expect to wear glasses (based on the probability in your class)? _____

6. How many students in your grade really do wear glasses? _____

7. Did the probability obtained from your class provide a good prediction for the entire grade? _____

Extension. Do you think that the probability figure from your class would be good to use to predict how many students in each grade at your school wear glasses? _____ Why or why not? _____
Check and see.

MATERIALS: paper, pencil.

DIFFERENT DICE

Not all dice are cubes. Get two dice like
these. They are called *octahedron dice.*

1. How many faces does each die have? _____
2. Make a list of the pairs of two numbers that
   can land up.

<u>1,1</u> <u>2,1</u> ___ ___ ___ ___ ___ ___ ___
<u>1,2</u> ___ ___ ___ ___ ___ ___ ___ ___
<u>1,3</u> ___ ___ ___ ___ ___ ___ ___ ___

___ ___ ___ ___ ___ ___ ___ ___

___ ___ ___ ___ ___ ___ ___ ___

___ ___ ___ ___ ___ ___ ___ ___

___ ___ ___ ___ ___ ___ ___ ___

___ ___ ___ ___ ___ ___ ___ ___

3. How many pairs are there altogether? _____
4. Write the sums for each pair in your list, below.
5. Which sum occurs most often? _____
6. a) How many times does a sum of 7 occur? _____
   b) Of 12? _____
   c) Of 1? _____
7. When you roll the dice, what is:
   a) Pr(sum of 7)? _____
   b) Pr(sum of 12)? _____
   c) Pr(sum of 5)? _____

Extension. Roll two octahedron dice 64 times. Keep a tally of the sums.
Find you *experimental probabilities* of rolling sums of 7, 12, and 5. Compare
these with the theoretical probabilities you found before.

MATERIALS: 2 octahedron dice, pencil.

AS THE TETRAHEDRON TUMBLES

A four-sided trianglular solid like this is
called a *tetrahedron*. Each of its four faces
is an equilateral triangle. A tetrahedron
die has four faces labeled:

When you roll a tetrahedron die, three faces will be up. You read the
number that is at the bottom of each of those three faces.
1. Try some rolls and record your results.
2. List the possible results when you roll a tetrahedron die: _____
3. How many are there? _____
4. Find the probabilities below:
   a) Pr(2) = _____
   b) Pr(4) = _____
   c) Pr(even number) = _____
   d) Pr(number less than 5) = _____
   e) Pr(square number) = _____

Now suppose we look at the face that is *down* and add the numbers that
are on that face.
5. List the possible sums: _____
6. How many are there? _____
7. Find the probabilities below:
   a) Pr(sum less than 6) = _____
   b) Pr(sum of 8) = _____
   c) Pr(sum greater than 10) = _____
   d) Pr(odd sum) = _____
   e) Pr(a sum that is a square) = _____

Extension. Roll a tetrahedron die 40 times and tally the sums of the numbers
on the face that lands down. Find experimental probabilities for the events
in problem 7 above. Compare them with the theoretical answers you found
before.

MATERIALS: one tetrahedron die, pencil, paper.

CHOOSING PAIRS

Choosing 2 people at a time from a group of 5 can be done many ways. The following people belong to a club and two bring refreshments each week: Ann, Bob, Carol, Diane, Eric.

1. Make a list of the possible pairs of members to bring refreshments. Use A for Ann, B for Bob, C for Carol, D for Diane, and E for Eric. Consider the pair A, B to be the same as B, A—it doesn't matter whose name comes first, they both have to bring refreshments.

_____ , _____   _____ , _____   _____ , _____

_____ , _____   _____ , _____   _____ , _____

_____ , _____   _____ , _____   _____ , _____

_____ , _____   _____ , _____   _____ , _____

2. How many weeks go by before the *same* two people would have to bring refreshments again? _____

3. If Frank joins the club, how many pairs can be made with the 6 people? _____
Make a list to find out.

MATERIALS: pencil.

THE DIE IS CAST

Suppose you roll one die.

1. List the possible results:_____

What is the probability that:
2. You roll a 6? _____

3. You roll a 2 or a 3? _____

4. You roll a 1, a 3, or a 5? _____

5. You roll a multiple of 3? _____

6. You roll a *prime number* (a number whose only divisor larger than 1 is itself)? _____

7. You roll a number 2 or larger? _____

8. You roll a number less than 4? _____

9. You roll a number less than 8? _____

10. You roll a fraction? _____

Extension. Toss a die 60 times and tally your results. Find your experimental probabilities for the events listed in problems 2–9. Compare these results with the theoretical answers you found before.

MATERIALS: pencil, one die.

WHO DO YOU BELIEVE?

Bill and Vicki are arguing over what happens when you flip two coins.

Bill says, "There are only three things that can happen. Both coins will be heads, just one will be a head, or they'll both be tails. Each thing should happen about 1/3 of the time."

Vicki replies, "No, Bill! Suppose you've got a dime and a quarter. They can both be heads, or *just the dime* is a head, or *just the quarter* is a head, or they're both tails. Each of these should happen about 1/4 of the time."

Bill says, "One of us is wrong. Let's each flip 2 coins 50 times. I'll write my results down my way and you write your results down your way. Let's see what happens."

1. Try the experiment with a partner. Use the tables below.

2. Who seems to be right? _____

Bill's Results

RESULT	TALLY	NUMBER OF TIMES
Both Heads		
One Head		
Both Tails		
TOTAL		50

Vicki's Results

RESULTS	TALLY	NUMBER OF TIMES
Both Heads		
Head on Dime (Tail on Quarter)		
Head on Quarter (Tail on Dime)		
Both Tails		
TOTAL		50

3. Why do you think so? _____

MATERIALS: 2 different coins, partner, pencil.

THE MULTIPLICATION PRINCIPLE

Aubrey drives from Sundown to Wagonwheel through Frontier City. There are 3 roads from Sundown to Frontier City and 4 roads from Frontier City to Wagonwheel. Aubrey gets bored if he drives the same way all the time. He wants to know all the possible ways from Sundown to Wagonwheel. To help him, he drew this picture:

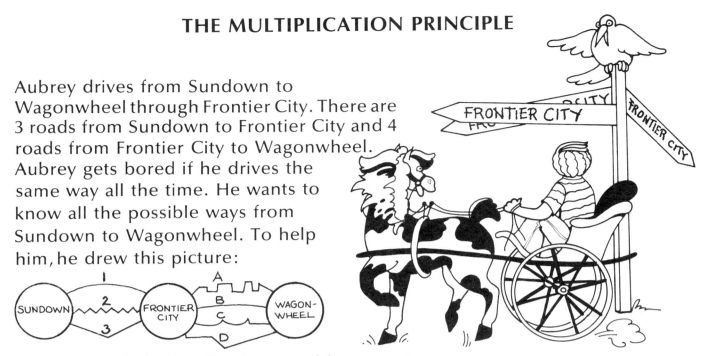

1. Can you help him list the possible routes?

1 A   2 A   3 A

Aubrey said "Wow! I have 12 different ways to drive to Wagonwheel from Sundown."

Aubrey showed the scheme to his friend Winnie. She said, "Sure there are 12 ways! You have 3 ways to get from Sundown to Frontier City. For each of those ways, you have 4 ways to get from Frontier City to Wagonwheel. And 3 × 4 = 12, so there are 12 ways in all."

Aubrey said, "Will multiplying always work?"

Winnie replied, "Sure. Suppose you have 5 shirts and 6 pairs of pants. You have 5 × 6 = 30 outfits you could wear. Some of them might look better than others, but they're all possible."

The method Winnie used is called the *multiplication principle*. If one thing can happen in *m* ways and then another thing can happen in *n* ways, there are *m* × *n* possible ways for both to happen.

MATERIALS: pencil.

USING THE MULTIPLICATION PRINCIPLE

The multiplication principle is a very important principle in probability. Use it in answering the exercises below. Make a list to check each problem.

1. At Pat's Pizza Parlor, there are 7 kinds of pizza meat and 5 other kinds of toppings. How many different pizza-topping creations could you eat? _____

2. The Trail Steak House has 2 kinds of salad, 5 kinds of steak, and 4 types of dessert.

a) How many different dinners could you order there, if a dinner includes a salad, a steak, and a dessert? _____

b) Without making a list find how many different meals you could order if they added 2 salads, 1 steak, and 1 dessert to the menu. _____

3. a) Lenny is a pilot. He has 2 cars he can drive to the airport. When he gets there, he has a choice of 6 airplanes to fly to another town for a meeting. When he arrives, any one of 3 taxicabs can pick him up to take him into town. How many different combinations of transportation are possible for his trip? _____

b) When Lenny returns, he can still catch any of the 3 taxicabs. However, he has to fly back the plane he brought. Then he has to drive home in the car he brought to the airport. How many combinations of transportation are possible for this trip home? _____

4. a) If you flip a dime and then flip a quarter, how many possible ways are there for the coins to land? _____

    b) List the ways: DIME   QUARTER

    c) What is the probability both land heads? _____

    d) What is the probability both land tails? _____

    e) What is the probability of one head and one tail? _____

MATERIALS: pencil.

FLIP AND TOSS

Suppose you flip a coin and then toss a die. What are the possibilities? You know the coin can land either heads or tails. And the die can land showing a 1, a 2, a 3, a 4, a 5, or a 6.

1. Complete the list of possibilities:

    H1   H2   ____   ____   ____   ____   ____
    T1   T2   ____   ____   ____   ____   ____

2. How may possibilities are there? _____

3. There are 2 ways a coin can land and 6 ways a die can land. Could you have used the multiplication rule to find the number of possibilities? _____

4. For this experiment, what is the probability of:
    a) A head? _____
    b) A head and a 3? _____
    c) A head and an even number? _____
    d) A tail? _____
    e) A tail and a prime number? _____
    f) A 2 or a 3? _____
    g) A 1, a 3, or a 5? _____
    h) A 4 or a 6? _____

Extension. Do this experiment 12 times. Record your results. Combine your results with a group or the whole class. Compare these results with the theoretical probabilities for problem 4.

MATERIALS: pencil, coin (optional), one die (optional).

TOOTHPASTE TOPS

Get a toothpaste top.
If you toss it, it can land 3 ways:

on its small end

on its side

on its large end

1. Toss the toothpaste top 50 times and record the results in the table below.

TOP LANDED ON	TALLY	NUMBER OF TIMES
Small End		
Side		
Large End		
TOTAL		50

2. What is the *experimental probability* of *your* toothpaste top landing on:
   a) Its small end? _____
   b) Its large end? _____
   c) Either end? _____
   d) Its side? _____

MATERIALS: toothpaste cap, pencil.

SUMMING SPINS

Use two spinners like these.

A 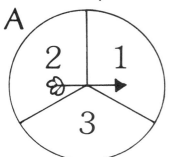   B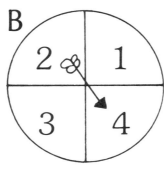

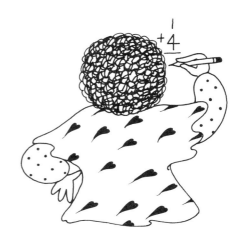

1. Spin each 24 times and record the result and their sums.

Spinner A																								
Spinner B																								

2.
   a) How many trials gave a *sum* of 3? _____ b) Of 4? _____ c) Of 5? _____

3. There were 24 trials in all.
   a) Find your experimental probability of spinning a sum of 3; _____
   b) a sum of 5; _____ .

4. List the possible outcomes for spinners A and B and the possible sums?

A, B	SUM	A, B	SUM	A, B	SUM
1, 1	2	2, 1			
1, 2	3				
1, 3	4				
1, 4					

5. Calculate the probability of each different sum.

6. Compare your *experimental probabilities* of Pr(sum of 3), Pr(sum of 5), with the theoretical probabilities of those events.

MATERIALS: spinners, pencil.

UNEVEN SPINNER

1. If you tried this spinner, would you expect any particular color more often than the others? _____

2. Which one? _____

You will need a spinner like the one above.

3. Try the spinner 24 times and tally the results.

COLOR	TALLY	NUMBER
Red		
Blue		
Green		
Black		
TOTAL		24

4. Write your *experimental* probabilities:
   a) experimental Pr(red) = _____
   b) experimental Pr(blue) = _____
   c) experimental Pr(green) = _____
   d) experimental Pr(black) = _____

Inspect the spinner carefully and compare the area of each color.

5. Assume red has a size of 1 and complete the table.

COLOR	SIZE
Red	1
Blue	
Green	
Black	

6. Write the *theoretical* probabilities:

a) Pr(red) = _____   c) Pr(green) = _____
b) Pr(blue) = _____   d) Pr(black) = _____

7. Find the differences between your experimental probabilities and the theoretical. Subtract the smaller fraction in each case.

a) Red _____   c) Black _____
b) Blue _____   d) Green _____

Extension. Combine your results with a group or the whole class. Find the differences between the experimental and theoretical probabilities again. Are they smaller? _____

MATERIALS: spinner, pencil.

HOW MANY ARE RED?

Ask your teacher for a paper bag containing twelve marbles.

DO NOT LOOK IN THE SACK!

1. Reach in and pull out a marble. Record its color in the table below. *Replace* the marble, shake the sack, and draw again. Do the experiment 24 or 36 times and keep a record.

COLOR	TALLY	NUMBER
Red		
Yellow		
Blue		
TOTAL		

2. How many red marbles do you think are in the sack? _____
Why? _____
3. Look and see. Were you close? _____

MATERIALS: pencil, bag of marbles.

WHAT ARE THE CHANCES OF YELLOW?

Choose a partner and ask your teacher for
the paper sack that goes with this experiment.
Be fair! Do not look inside the sack.

EXPERIMENT

1. The sack contains red, yellow, and blue cubes. Reach in the sack,
take out a cube, and record its color in the table below. *Replace* the cube,
shake up the sack, and draw again. Do this experiment 24 times.

COLOR	TALLY	NUMBER
Red		
Yellow		
Blue		
TOTAL		24

2. Write your *experimental probabilities:*
   a) Pr(red) = _____
   b) Pr(yellow) = _____
   c) Pr(blue) = _____

3. If the sack contained 24 cubes, how many of each color would you guess
are in the sack? a) Red _____, b) Yellow _____, c) Blue _____

4. If there were 12 cubes, then there would be a) _____ red, b) _____ yellow,
and c) _____ blue.

Now look in the sack and see how many of each color there are.

ANOTHER EXPERIMENT

Ask your teacher to change the cubes in the sack and perform the
experiment again. *Don't peek!*

5. Draw 20 times and record your results on another paper.

6. Which color did you draw most often this time? _____

7. How many of each color do you think are in the sack? _____

8. If you had to guess the color before drawing, what color would you
choose? _____

9. What is the experimental probability of your choice for the guess based
on the results of your experiment? _____

10. Look in the sack and compare your experimental results with the actual
cubes. Were you right? _____

MATERIALS: pencil, 2 bags of color cubes.

CHANGING PROBABILITY

A gumball machine contains 100 balls:
50 red, 20 green, 10 blue, 15 yellow, 5 with
white stars.

Each costs 1¢, but if you get a gumball with
white stars, you can exchange it for a 5¢
jawbreaker.

1. Find these probabilities for a full gumball machine:
   a) Pr(red) = _____
   b) Pr(blue) = _____
   c) Pr(white stars) = _____
   d) Pr(jawbreaker) = _____

2. If a lot of neighborhood kids bought gumballs from the machine before you
got there, how would that affect your chances to win a jawbreaker? _____
_____

3. Suppose the kids got 20 red, 8 green, 1 blue, 4 yellow, and 1 white.
What is your chance for a jawbreaker now? _____

4. Would it be cheaper to spend 100¢ to get all the gumballs in order to have
all of the jawbreakers, or just to buy the jawbreakers? _____
Why? _____

MATERIALS: pencil.

HOW MUCH DOES PROBABILITY CHANGE?

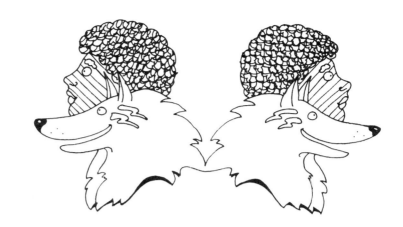

Activities 49 and 50 looked at probability in two ways.

I. The gumball machine used probability calculated *without replacing* the gumballs.

II. In the marble experiment you *replaced* the marble after each draw.

Would it have mattered if you could put the gumballs back in the machine?
Would it have mattered if you kept the marbles out after drawing?
Think about the marble problem. Remember there were 10 red, 6 yellow, and 4 blue marbles in the container.
1. Fill in the table below.

PR(RED MARBLE)

Trial	Replace Marble	Don't Replace Marble	Color Drawn
1			Yellow
2			Blue
3			Yellow
4			

2. Suppose you draw a red first and don't put it back.
What's the probability of getting a red on the next draw? _____
3. Does replacement make a difference? _____

MATERIALS: pencil, container with 10 red, 6 yellow, and 4 blue marbles (optional).

TREASURE CHEST

Twenty students' names are in the treasure chest drawing.

There are two prizes: a stuffed animal and a transistor radio.

On Friday, two names will be drawn. If your name is in the Treasure Chest, what will your chances be?

1. First, what questions should be asked in order to write the probability? Consider the number of prizes and the number of names.

2. How would replacing names affect the drawing? _____
_____

3. Write the probabilities for your winning on Friday. Assume that names are replaced.
   a) Pr(you win on first draw) _____
   b) Pr(you win on second draw) _____

4. Now assume names are not replaced. What is:
   a) Pr(you win on first draw)? _____
   b) Pr(you win on second draw)? _____

5. Under what circumstances could you win both prizes? _____
_____

6. What is that probability? _____

MATERIALS: pencil.

TREAT BY PHONE

HALLOWEEN TREAT

Girls and Boys: The City Tigers Club is sponsoring a Halloween Night Treat. You may win a bicycle or some money. Here is how to win!

Halloween Night: Be at home by 8:00 P.M. Names will be drawn and those students called. If they are home they will win a prize.

Prizes to be Given: A city wide drawing for two bicycles. One is given to a student in grades 1–3; the second bicycle to a student in grades 4–6.

Each school will have a drawing for grades K–6, and three $5 prizes will be awarded.

For your city and school, find out the probability of your winning a Halloween Treat Prize.

1. What information will you need to know to figure this out? _____
_____

2. How will you go about finding this information? _____
_____

3. What is your probability of winning $5? _____

4. What is your probability of winning a bicycle? _____

MATERIALS: pencil.

PENNY TOSS

Vicki, Dee, and Linda are playing a coin game. Each tosses a penny. Score is kept as follows.

Vicki gets a point if all three coins are heads. Dee gets a point if all three coins land tails. Linda gets a point if there is a mixture of heads and tails.

The game ends when one player gets 30 points.

1. List the possible outcomes from tossing the pennies. Keep them in order: Vicki, Dee, then Linda.

H H H	T H H	_____
H H T	_____	_____
H T H	_____	_____
H T T	_____	_____

2. How many possible outcomes are there according to the multiplication rule? _____

3. Does this check with your list? _____

4. What are the chances of Vicki getting a point on the first flip? _____

5. What are Linda's chances on the first flip? _____

6. What are Dee's chances? _____

7. Will these probabilities change as the game goes on? _____

8. Who is most likely to win the game? _____

9. Is this a fair game? _____

10. If not, how can points be assigned to make it a fair game?

MATERIALS: 3 pennies, pencil, paper.

THREE COINS ON THE TABLE

Remember that 1 coin can land 2 ways
(heads or tails). Two coins can land 4 ways:

H H   H T   T H   T T

1. How many ways can three coins land? _____
2. List the ways on another paper.
3. How many ways can four coins land? _____
4. List the ways on another paper.
5. If four coins are tossed, what is the probability of:
   a) 4 heads? _____
   b) 2 heads, 2 tails? _____
   c) 1 head, 3 tails? _____
   d) 4 tails? _____
   e) 1 or 2 or 3 heads? _____
   f) no tails? _____
6. How many ways are there for 5 coins to land? _____
7.
   a) How many ways are there for 6 coins to land? _____
   b) What is the probability that, if 6 coins are tossed, they will *all* be
heads? _____
8. Is there a pattern to the number of ways coins can land? _____
9. Could you use the multiplication rule here? _____

Extension. Suppose the probability of having a child that is a boy is 1/2 and
a girl 1/2.
For a two child family, what is the probability of 2 girls? _____ A boy and a
girl? _____ A girl *then* a boy? _____
Make up probability questions for larger families and find the answers.

MATERIALS: pencil, paper, pennies (optional).

FOUR COINS

Select four coins that you can distinguish such as a penny, nickel, dime, and quarter. Shake them in a paper cup and spill them onto a flat surface. Think of the possible outcomes of this experiment and list them on another sheet of paper or use your list from Activity 55.

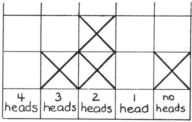

1. How many possible outcomes are there? _____
2. What is the probability of each possibility? _____
3. Theoretically, you would expect HHHH to occur in 1 out of 16 trials on the average.
    a) In how many out of 32? _____
    b) Out of 64? _____
    c) Out of 80? _____
4. How frequently in 80 trials would you expect:
    a) 4 heads? _____   d) 1 head? _____
    b) 3 heads? _____   e) All tails? _____
    c) 2 heads? _____
5. Perform the experiment 80 times and tally the outcomes according to the number of heads.
6. Make a bar graph of your outcomes. Use one bar for each of the possibilities: 4 heads, 2 heads, 1 head, all tails. It will look something like the one below. Mark the expected results on your graph, too. Color the number of squares expected for each outcome red.

7. How does your graph compare to what you expected?_____
8. Combine your results with ten classmates. Make a new bar graph for your whole class.
9. Combining results with classmates provides a large number of trials for the experiment. How did having a larger number of trials affect the comparison? _____
10. Are the new results closer to what you expected originally than just yours alone? _____

MATERIALS: 4 coins, graph paper, red crayon, paper, pencil.

FAMILY MEMBERS

Take a survey of your class to find out the numbers of brothers, sisters, and pets your classmates have.

1. Tally the results in the table below.

	0	1	2	3	More
Brothers					
Sisters					
Cats					
Dogs					

Total number of students: _____

2. Use the information to find the experimental probabilities for the events in the table for your class. Write them in the table below.

	Pr(0)	Pr(1)	Pr(2)	Pr(3)	Pr(More than 3)
Brothers					
Sisters					
Cats					
Dogs					

3. Find out the enrollment of two other classes. Make predictions about the numbers of brothers, sisters, and pets they have using the experimental probabilities from your class. Make a table of your predictions for each class.
4. Select one or two students to go to those classes and find the actual results. First ask your teacher to make arrangements with the other teachers.
5. Write a few sentences about what you found on another paper.

Extension. Predict the results for 50 students. Select two or three students to go to the cafeteria during lunch and gather the information from 50 students. Be sure to include strangers in the survey, too. Write a short paragraph about what you learned.

MATERIALS: pencil, paper.

DICE NUMBERS

You have learned that when two dice are rolled, there are 36 different possibilities. Usually when you play a dice game, you add the spots on the top faces. The possible outcomes are the numbers from 2 to 12.

To be different, roll a red die and a white die. Read the result as a two-digit number, with the red number as the tens digit. If you roll red 5 and white 3, read it as 53. This will give you 36 different numbers. Call these *dice numbers.*

In the table below, some of the dice numbers are filled in.

1. Complete the table.

White Die

	1	2	3	4	5	6
1	11	12	13	14		
2						
3	31				35	
4			44			
5	51					
6						66

Red Die (label on left side)

2. How many of the numbers are over 50? _____
3. What is the probability of rolling a number over 50? _____
4. What is the probability of rolling a number under 40? _____
5. What is the probability of rolling a double? _____
(33 and 55 are doubles—there are others) _____
6. What is the probability of rolling an even number? _____
7. What is the probability of rolling a number with both digits even? _____
8. List the possible primes: _____
9. What is the probability of rolling a prime number? _____
10. What is the probability of rolling a number where each digit is a prime? _____
List these numbers first: _____
11. What is the probability that the number has a 4 as at least one of its digits? _____
12. What is the probability that the number is a multiple of 6? _____

MATERIALS: pencil, two dice (one red, one white—optional).

DODECAHEDRON AND ICOSAHEDRON DICE

A *dodecahedron* looks like this:

It has 12 faces. To use it as a die, the faces are numbered 1 to 12. (Because of the 12 faces, dodecahedra are sometimes used as paperweight calendars).

An *icosahedron* looks like this:

It has 20 faces. Sometimes, to make a die out of an icosahedron, the faces are numbered 0 to 9, with two faces having each number.
If you roll the dodecahedron first and the
icosahedron next and write the top numbers
as one number, like this:

Dodecahedron   Icosahedron

you have 84. Sometimes you get a three-
digit number and sometimes a two-digit
number.
1. How many numbers are possible altogether? _____
Hint. Use the multiplication rule.
Here is an example of a three-digit number:

Dodecahedron   Icosahedron

2. What has to happen to cause a three-digit number?_____
3. How many ways can you roll a three-digit number? _____
4. What is the probability of rolling a three-digit number? _____
5. Could you roll a four-digit number? _____
6. Ask your teacher for a dodecahedron die and an icosahedron die. Toss them 50 times. Keep track of the number of three-digit numbers you rolled.
   a) How many three-digit numbers did you expect? _____
   b) How many three-digit numbers did you roll? _____
   c) What is your experimental probability of rolling a three-digit number? _____
   d) Write about your results on the back of this paper.

MATERIALS: one dodecahedron die, one icosahedron die, pencil.

ICE CREAM

Three popular flavors of ice cream are chocolate, strawberry, and vanilla. Take a class survey. Find out which of the three flavors of ice cream each student prefers.

1. Based on the class sample, fill in the table below.

FAVORITE FLAVOR	NUMBER PICKING THE FLAVOR	EXPERIMENTAL PROBABILITY THE FLAVOR IS PICKED
Chocolate		
Strawberry		
Vanilla		
TOTAL		

2. Now choose two or three students from your class to take the same survey at lunch time. Have them ask at least 20 students and share the results with the class. Were the lunch survey results similar to your class results? _____
How do you explain this? _____
_____
_____

3. Now have the survey takers ask at least 20 more students their favorite ice cream flavors, but this time they may pick any flavor (not just chocolate, strawberry or vanilla).
Make a table of the results and find the experimental probabilities for each flavor.
4. How do these results differ from the first ones? _____
_____
_____

MATERIALS: paper, pencil.

TO THE ICE CREAM SHOPPE

Sally and Jack went to the ICE CREAM SHOPPE. It has only three flavors (vanilla, chocolate, and strawberry), but the ice cream is good, the price is low, and if the owner likes you, he gives you BIG scoops.

Sally wonders, "How many different double-dip cones are possible?"

Jack: "Does it matter which flavor is on top?"

Sally: "Sure—chocolate melting down on vanilla is different from vanilla running over chocolate."

Jack: "Then there are 9—three possible on top, and three possible on the bottom: $3 \times 3 = 9$."

Here they are:

1. What is the probability at least one of the scoops is chocolate? _____
2. What is the probability that neither scoop is vanilla? _____
3. What is the probability that both scoops are the same flavor? _____
4. What is the probability that both scoops are strawberry? _____
5. If a vanilla scoop costs 10¢, and the other flavors cost 15¢ a scoop, what is the probability a double-dip cone will cost 30¢? _____

MATERIALS: pencil.

WATCHING THE WEATHER

1. Cloudy Jim, the weatherman, predicts a 30% chance of rain tomorrow! What is the chance it will not rain tomorrow? _____

2. a) If Cloudy Jim predicts a 30% chance of rain for 10 days in a row, about how many of those days would you expect it to rain? _____ Why? _____

_____

   b) If it actually rained 4 days in that period, would you be surprised? _____

3. How big would the chance of rain have to be before you wouldn't plan a picnic? _____

4. a) If Cloudy Jim said the chance of rain was 5% each day for 20 days, and it rained 1 day in that time, would you be surprised? _____ Why or why not? _____

   b) Would you say, "What a dumb weatherman!" on the day it rained? _____

Why or why not? _____

_____

Extension. Check the weather records for your area. Determine the (experimental) probability of rain for each month. Determine how many days of each month you would expect to be rainy.
Make a graph of the expected number of rainy days for each month.
Do this for a desert and a rainy region of the world (for example, Central Australia and Central Kauai, Hawaii). Discuss the results.

MATERIALS: pencil, paper, almanac.

A SACK OF MARBLES

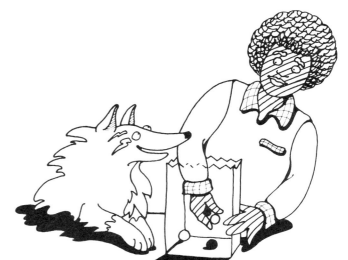

A paper bag contains 2 red and 2 green marbles. You are to take out one at a time until the bag is empty.

1. List the orders in which you can remove the marbles.

2. What is Pr(green then red)? _____
3. What is Pr(red then green)? _____
4. What is Pr(removing two green in a row)? _____
5. What is Pr(the colors will alternate)? _____

NOW DO THE EXPERIMENT.
6. Draw all of the marbles out 25 times and list the outcomes by color. Use R for red and G for green on another paper.
7. Calculate your experimental probabilities for the events in problems 1–4 above.
8. How do your results compare with the theoretical probabilities you calculated above?

Extension. Combine your results with a group or the whole class. Compare the combined experimental probabilities with the theoretical ones.

MATERIALS: pencil, paper bag, 2 red and 2 green marbles, paper.

A GOOD MEAL?

Susan's little brother was very mischievous.
He climbed into the canned food cupboard
and pulled off all of the soup and meat
can labels! Fortunately, he did not move
the cans off their shelves, and Susan found
all of the labels.

She found the following labels:

   Soup: 2 vegetable, 1 tomato, 3 chicken noodle, 1 beef, and 2 mushroom;
   Meat: 2 tuna fish, 1 Spam, 2 corned beef, and 1 salmon.

1. How many soups are there altogether? _____

2. How many meats? _____

3. How many pairs of soup and meat? _____

Hint. Use the multiplication rule.

4. If Susan chooses a soup, what is the probability she will pick chicken
noodle? _____

5. What are her chances of eating a corned beef sandwich? _____

6. What is Pr(mushroom soup)? _____

7. What is the number of ways for Susan to have tomato soup and a Spam
sandwich? _____

8. How many ways are there for her to eat a tuna fish sandwich and tomato
soup? _____

9. What is Pr(mushroom soup and salmon)? _____

10. What is Pr(her choice of soup and meat)? _____

11. Suppose 2 more cans of tomato soup and 1 of Spam are found and
added to the shelves. Now what is the probability of having tomato soup
and Spam? _____

MATERIALS: pencil.

ROADS AND HIGHWAYS

The map shows the highways and roads
connecting Deerborn, Rundell, and LaPorta.

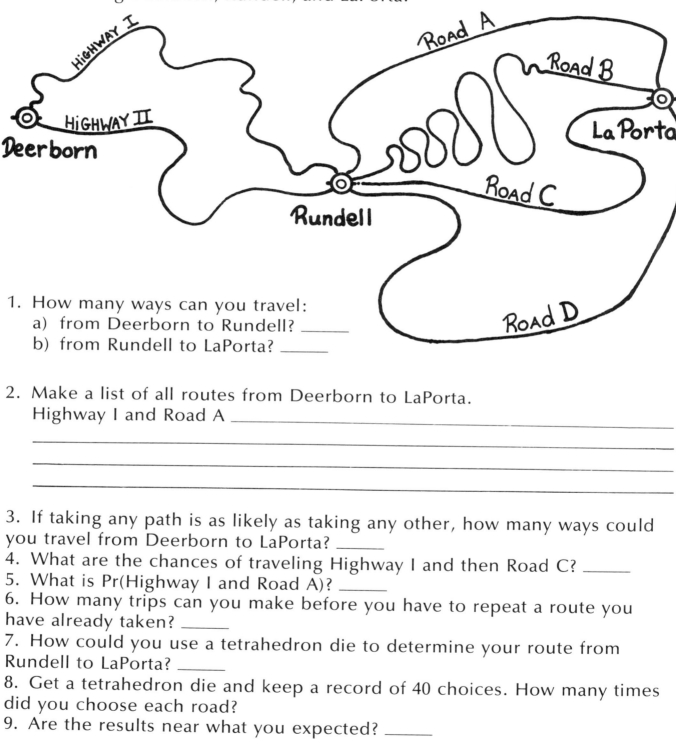

1. How many ways can you travel:
   a) from Deerborn to Rundell? _____
   b) from Rundell to LaPorta? _____

2. Make a list of all routes from Deerborn to LaPorta.
   Highway I and Road A _____
   _____
   _____
   _____

3. If taking any path is as likely as taking any other, how many ways could
you travel from Deerborn to LaPorta? _____
4. What are the chances of traveling Highway I and then Road C? _____
5. What is Pr(Highway I and Road A)? _____
6. How many trips can you make before you have to repeat a route you
have already taken? _____
7. How could you use a tetrahedron die to determine your route from
Rundell to LaPorta? _____
8. Get a tetrahedron die and keep a record of 40 choices. How many times
did you choose each road?
9. Are the results near what you expected? _____

MATERIALS: tetrahedron die, pencil.

WHAT ARE THE CHANCES?

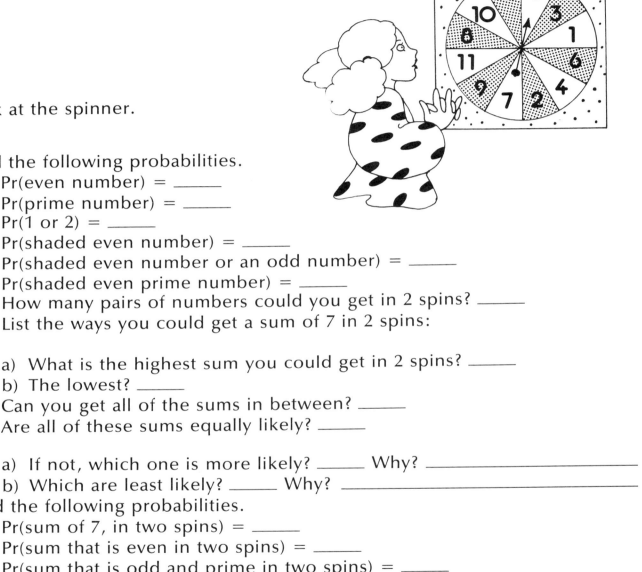

Look at the spinner.

Find the following probabilities.
1. Pr(even number) = _____
2. Pr(prime number) = _____
3. Pr(1 or 2) = _____
4. Pr(shaded even number) = _____
5. Pr(shaded even number or an odd number) = _____
6. Pr(shaded even prime number) = _____
7. How many pairs of numbers could you get in 2 spins? _____
8. List the ways you could get a sum of 7 in 2 spins:

9. a) What is the highest sum you could get in 2 spins? _____
   b) The lowest? _____
10. Can you get all of the sums in between? _____
11. Are all of these sums equally likely? _____

12. a) If not, which one is more likely? _____ Why? _____
    b) Which are least likely? _____ Why? _____
Find the following probabilities.
13. Pr(sum of 7, in two spins) = _____
14. Pr(sum that is even in two spins) = _____
15. Pr(sum that is odd and prime in two spins) = _____
16. Pr(not spinning a sum that is a factor of 66 in two spins) = _____

MATERIALS: pencil, spinner (optional).

THE FIRST ACE PROBLEM

There are 4 aces in a regular deck of 52 cards.

1. If you shuffle the cards thoroughly and turn them over one by one, how many cards would you expect to turn over on the average before you get an ace? _____

2. Try this 10 times and record the number of cards you turn over *before* you get an ace.

Trial	Number of Cards *Before* First Ace
1	
2	
3	
4	
5	
6	
7	
8	
9	
10	
Total	

3. Calculate the average.
Average _____

4. How close was this to your prediction? _____
Ask your teacher to help you work out the real average.

MATERIALS: regular deck of playing cards, pencil.

FINDING THE GREEN MARBLE

Put 10 marbles (9 blue and 1 green) in a
bag. Shake the bag and draw a marble
without looking. If the marble is green, *stop*.
If the marble is blue, put it aside and draw
again. Continue until you draw the green
marble.

1. How many draws do you think it will take to find the green marble? _____
2. What is the most draws it could take? _____
3. Do this experiment 10 times. Keep track each time of how many draws it
takes to draw the green marble. Put this information in the table below.

Experiment Number	Number of Draws
1	
2	
3	
4	
5	
6	
7	
8	
9	
10	
Total	

4. Find the average number of draws to get a green:

$$\text{Average Number of Draws} = \frac{\text{Total Number of Draws}}{10} = \underline{\hspace{3cm}}$$

MATERIALS: pencil, marbles (9 blue, 1 green).

HOW'S THE MARKET?

Take the page in the newspaper that lists stocks from the New York Stock Exchange.

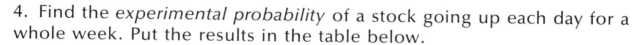

1. How many stocks went up in value? (This is shown by a + in the last column.) _____

2. How many stocks went down in value? (This is shown by a − in the last column.) _____

3. On this day, what was the *experimental probability* of a stock going up? _____

4. Find the *experimental probability* of a stock going up each day for a whole week. Put the results in the table below.

Day	Probability Stock Went Up
1	
2	
3	
4	
5	

5. Did the probabilities stay pretty much the same, or did they change a lot?
_____

6. What do you think caused the changes? _____

7. Do you think probability would be very useful in predicting things in the stock market? _____

Why or why not? _____

Extension. Use your experimental probabilities to predict how stocks will go up the same day next week. Check next week to see how close your prediction was.

MATERIALS: newspaper stock report, pencil.

THE THREE DICE

1. Put three dice in a cup, shake them well, and toss them onto a table. Add the numbers on their top faces. Do this 100 times and tally the results in the table below. Find your experimental probabilities. Change them to decimal form. (Do you know the easy way to do this?) Then fill in the third column.

Sum	Tally	Number of Times	Probability from Experiment	Theoretical Probability
3				0.005
4				0.014
5				0.028
6				0.046
7				0.069
8				0.097
9				0.116
10				0.125
11				0.125
12				0.116
13				0.097
14				0.069
15				0.046
16				0.028
17				0.014
18				0.005
TOTAL		100		1.000

2. How do you feel about your results? Are they close enough to the theoretical probabilities? _____

3. Do you think your dice are fair? _____

4. What could you do to have your results come closer to the theoretical probabilities? _____

5. Can you explain how the theoretical probabilities were calculated? _____

MATERIALS: 3 dice, paper cup, pencil.

GAME OF DIGITS

Choose two partners. Call yourselves A, B, and C.
Play the following game: On the count of three each of you extends either 1, 2, or 3 fingers on one hand.
A gets 1 point if all three match, B gets 1 point if two people match, and C gets 1 point if there are no matches.
1. Try the game 27 times and keep a record of points.

	Tally	Total
A		
B		
C		

2. According to your record, does the game seem fair? _____
3. Which player would you like to be A, B, or C? _____
4. List the possible outcomes for the game on another sheet of paper.
5. Find the probabilities for each person winning:
a) Pr(A winning) = _____ ; b) Pr(B winning) = _____ ; c) Pr(C winning) = _____ .
6. Is there a fairer way to assign points for winning? _____
Try to make a *fair* Game of Digits. Write *your* rules here.

MATERIALS: paper, pencil.

NAME THE CONTAINER

You will need a partner, 5 containers,
and 75 red and 75 blue marbles (or counters).
Put your marbles into the containers
according to the rule your teacher gives
you.
Mix up the order of the containers so
your partner does not know their contents,
except that each contains 30 marbles.

1. Ask your partner to choose a container and draw 15 marbles from it,
one at a time, using replacement. Record the color of each; use R for red
and B for blue.

Drawing	1	2	3	4	5	6	7	8	9	10	11	12	13	14	15
Color															

2. Now have your partner guess the number of red and blue marbles in
the container:
    a) _____ red;   b) _____ blue.
Check the guess.

3. Do you think the guesses would be better or worse after drawing
without replacement?

4. What would be the effect of selecting only 10 marbles, or as many as
20 marbles? _____

5. Are the probabilities of guessing correctly increased or decreased as the
number of selections is changed? _____

6. Try this experiment again with only 10 drawings.

Now it's your turn to draw from your partner and guess.

MATERIALS: partner, 150 marbles each (75 blue and 75 red), 5 containers,
pencil.

A WORLD RECORD

A game about world records has this contest for players. Who can set a record for the most rolls of 2 dice *without* getting doubles?

The record book comes with the game and as records are broken, the person's name is entered as the new record holder.

1. Try the challenge. Roll two dice and write down the number of rolls you can make without getting doubles. Do the feat 25 times.

Try	Number of Rolls	Try	Number of Rolls
1		13	
2		14	
3		15	
4		16	
5		17	
6		18	
7		19	
8		20	
9		21	
10		22	
11		23	
12		24	
		25	

2. Does there seem to be a limit to the number of rolls you can make before getting a double? _____

3. Do you think it would be rare for the number of rolls to reach 40? _____

4. Consider the outcomes when rolling dice and the probability of getting a double. Explain why rolling a large number of times without getting double is a fantastic feat and deserves world recognition.

MATERIALS: 2 dice, pencil.

SOLUTIONS

Activity 1
1. 25
2.–4. Answers will vary.

Activity 2
1. Answers will vary.
2. Guess Y.
3. Answers will vary.
4. More difficult—equal probabilities.
5. See 4.
6. No. Guess colors or numbers only.

Activity 3
1. 9
2. 9
3. 9
4.–6. Answers will vary.

Activity 4
1. 25 25 25 25
2. 20 20 20 20 20
3. 10 (ten times)

Activity 5
1.–2. Answers will vary.
3.

Blue	Red	Yellow
Blue	Yellow	Red
Red	Blue	Yellow
Red	Yellow	Blue
Yellow	Red	Blue
Yellow	Blue	Red

4. 6
5. 5
6. 1

Activity 6
1.

Coke	Pepsi	RC Cola
Coke	RC Cola	Pepsi
Pepsi	Coke	RC Cola
Pepsi	RC Cola	Coke
RC Cola	Coke	Pepsi
RC Cola	Pepsi	Coke

2. 6
3. 4
4. 1/6 × number of students in class
5. Answers will vary.
6.–8. Answers will vary by class.

Activity 7
1.–2. Answers will vary.

Activity 8
1.–2. Answers will vary.

Activity 9
1. 1/2
2. 1/3
3. 1/6

Activity 10
1a. 6; b. 1,2,3,4,5,6
2. 1
3. 3;   1,3,5
4. 3;   3/6 or 1/2
5a. 4/6 or 2/3; b. 1/6; c. 3/6 or 1/2; d. 5/6
6. 4
7a. 1/4; b. 1/4; c. 1/4; d. 1/4
8. 10
9a. 2/10 or 1/5; b. 2/10 or 1/5; c. 5/10 or 1/2; d. 1/10
10. The outcomes in problem 3 are not equally likely.

Activity 11
1. Pr(tail) or Pr(T)
2. Pr(blue)
3. Pr(even number)
4. Pr(ace)
5. The probability of tossing a tail when tossing a coin equals 1/2.
6. The probability of rolling a 3 on a die equals 1/6.
7. The probability of spinning yellow or blue on the spinner above equals 2/3.
8. The probability of making a hit in a baseball game equals .300.
9. The probability of rain is 40%.

Activity 12
1. I
2. P
3. P
4. C
5. P
6. I
7. P
8. C
9. P
10. P
11. Answers will vary.
12. 0
13. 1

Activity 13
1a. 1/4; b. 1/4; c. 3/4; d. 2/4 or 1/2; e. 1; f. 0
2a. 1/6; b. 3/6 or 1/2; c. 0; d. 1; e. 1/6; f. 5/6; g. 1
3. 1
4. certain
5. 0
6. 2/3
7. 2/7

Activity 14
1.–2. Answers will vary.
3. no question
4. 1/6
5. 1,2,3,4,5,6;   1/6;   5/6

Activity 15
1a. 1/4; b. 1/2; c. 8/9; d. 0.4; e. 0.46; f. 1/8; g. 0.90; h. 1
2a. 1/3; b. 0.1; c. 0.7; d. 2/5; e. 1; f. 7/9; g. 1/2; h. 0.44; i. 0.88
3. Subtract the given probability from 1.

Activity 16
1. 26%
2. .653
3. 1/3
4. 8/10 or 4/5
5. His past record is about 60% successes, so you might say he has a fair chance, but not excellent.
6. 1/2
7. 2/5
8. 25%

Activity 17
1. 10; there are 10 equally likely numbers.
2.–3. Answers will vary.

Activity 18
1.–7. Answers will vary.

Activity 19
1. 200
2.–3. Answers will vary.
4. Answers will vary by class.

Activity 20
1.–6. Answers will vary.

Activity 21
1.–4. Answers will vary.
5. No.
6. No.

Activity 22
1.–5. Answers will vary.

Activity 23
1. Most students will answer 25.
2. Answers will vary.
3. No.
4. Answers will vary.

Activity 24
1.–9. Answers will vary.

Activity 25
1.–9. Answers will vary.

Activity 26
1.   1,1 2,1 3,1 4,1 5,1 6,1
    1,2 2,2 3,2 4,2 5,2 6,2
    1,3 2,3 3,3 4,3 5,3 6,3
    1,4 2,4 3,4 4,4 5,4 6,4
    1,5 2,5 3,5 4,5 5,5 6,5
    1,6 2,6 3,6 4,6 5,6 6,6
2. 6
3. 6
4. 36
5. 2; 12
6. Yes.
7. 2, 3, 4, 5, 6, 7,
   8, 9, 10, 11, 12
8. Yes. Answers will vary.
9. Answers will vary.
10a. 1; 6+6; **b.** 2; 5+6, 6+5;
   c. 0; **d.** 5; 2+6, 6+2,
   3+5, 5+3, 4+4
11. 7
12a. 1/36; **b.** 5/36; **c.** 6/36
   or 1/6; **d.** 4/36 or 1/9;
   e. 8/36 or 2/9; **f.** 10/36 or
   5/18;

Activity 27
1. 36
2. 1+6, 6+1, 2+5, 5+2, 3+4,
   4+3
3. 6/36 or 1/6
4a. 1/36; **b.** 5/36; **c.** 3/36 or
   1/12; **d.** 1/36; **e.** 2/36 or
   1/18; **f.** 6/36 or 1/6
5.–8. Answers will vary.

Activity 28
1. 6
2. 16 or 17
3.–4. Answers will vary.

Activity 29
1.–3. Answers will vary.

Activity 30
1a. 3/10; **b.** 4/10 or 2/5;
   c. 2/10 or 1/5; **d.** 1/10
2.–3. Answers will vary.

Activity 31
1.–2. Answers will vary.
3. 10/20 or 1/2;
4.–5. Answers will vary.

Activity 32
1a. 1/3; **b.** 1/3; **c.** 2/3
2. blue, green; blue, red;
   red, green
3. 3
4a. 1/3; **b.** 1/3; **c.** 1/3
5a. 1/4; **b.** 2/4 or 1/2;
   c. 2/4 or 1/2
6. blue, green; blue, red $_1$;
   blue, red $_2$; green, red $_1$;
   green, red $_2$; red $_1$, red $_2$
7a. 1/6; **b.** 1/6; **c.** 2/6 or 1/3

Activity 33
1. 1
2. 2
3. tomato soup   tomato soup
   steak   chicken
   pudding   pudding

   tomato soup   tomato soup
   steak   chicken
   cake   cake

   onion soup   onion soup
   steak   chicken
   pudding   pudding

   onion soup   onion soup
   steak   chicken
   cake   cake
4a. 24; **b.** 60
5. Answers will vary.
6. Use the multiplication rule.

Activity 34
1. 25
2. 1/2
3.–5. Answers will vary.
6. HH, HT, TH, TT
7. 1/2
8. Answers will vary.

Activity 35
1. Answers will vary.
2. E is the most likely answer.
3. Probably.
4a.–**b.** E is the most likely answer.
  c. Q, X, or Z are the most likely
     answers.

Activity 36
1.–7. Answers will vary.

Activity 37
1. 8
2. 1,1   2,1   3,1   4,1
    1,2   2,2   3,2   4,2
    1,3   2,3   3,3   4,3
    1,4   2,4   3,4   4,4
    1,5   2,5   3,5   4,5
    1,6   2,6   3,6   4,6
    1,7   2,7   3,7   4,7
    1,8   2,8   3,8   4,8
    5,1   6,1   7,1   8,1
    5,2   6,2   7,2   8,2
    5,3   6,3   7,3   8,3
    5,4   6,4   7,4   8,4
    5,5   6,5   7,5   8,5
    5,6   6,6   7,6   8,6
    5,7   6,7   7,7   8,7
    5,8   6,8   7,8   8,8
3. 64
4. 2   3   4   5   6   7   8   9
    3   4   5   6   7   8   9 10
    4   5   6   7   8   9 10 11
    5   6   7   8   9 10 11 12
    6   7   8   9 10 11 12 13
    7   8   9 10 11 12 13 14
    8   9 10 11 12 13 14 15
    9 10 11 12 13 14 15 16
5. 9
6a. 6; **b.** 5; **c.** 0
7a. 6/64 or 3/32; **b.** 5/64;
   c. 4/64 or 1/16

Activity 38
1. Answers will vary.
2. 1, 2, 3, 4
3. 4
4a. 1/4; **b.** 1/4; **c.** 2/4 or 1/2.
   d. 1; **e.** 2/4 or 1/2
5. 6, 7, 8, 9
6. 4
7a. 0; **b.** 1/4; **c.** 0; **d.** 2/4
   or 1/2; **e.** 1/4

Activity 39
1. A,B   A,C   A,D   A,E
   B,C   B,D   B,E
   C,D   C,E
   D,E
2. 10
3. 15

Activity 40
1. 1, 2, 3, 4, 5, 6
2. 1/6
3. 2/6 or 1/3
4. 3/6 or 1/2
5. 2/6 or 1/3
6. 3/6 or 1/2; one is not a prime number.
7. 5/6
8. 3/6 or 1/2
9. 1
10. 0

Activity 41
1. Answers will vary.
2. It should be Vicki.
3. The outcomes in Bill's table are not equally likely.

Activity 42
1. 1A   1B   1C   1D
   2A   2B   2C   2D
   3A   3B   3C   3D

Activity 43
1. 35
2a. 40; b. 120
3a. 36; b. 3
4a. 4;
  b.

DIME	QUARTER
H	H
H	T
T	H
T	T

  c. 1/4; d. 1/4; e. 2/4 or 1/2

Activity 44
1. H1 H2 H3 H4 H5 H6
   T1 T2 T3 T4 T5 T6
2. 12
3. Yes; 2 × 6 = 12.
4a. 6/12 or 1/2; b. 1/12;
  c. 3/12 or 1/4; d. 6/12 or 1/2; e. 3/12 or 1/4;
  f. 4/12 or 1/3; g. 6/12 or 1/2; h. 4/12 or 1/3

Activity 45
1.–2. Answers will vary.

Activity 46
1.–3. Answers will vary.
4.

OUTCOMES				SUMS		
1,1	1,2	1,3	1,4	2	3	4	5
2,1	2,2	2,3	2,4	3	4	5	6
3,1	3,2	3,3	3,4	4	5	6	7

5. Pr(2) = 1/12; Pr(3) = 2/12 = 1/6; Pr(4) = 3/12 = 1/4; Pr(5) = 3/12 = 1/4; Pr(6) = 2/12 = 1/6; Pr(7) = 1/12
6. Answers will vary.

Activity 47
1. Yes.
2. Green.
3.–4. Answers will vary.
5. Red   1
   Blue   2
   Green 3
   Black 2
6a. 1/8; b. 2/8 or 1/4; c. 3/8;
  d. 2/8 or 1/4
7. Answers will vary.

Activity 48
1.–3. Answers will vary.

Activity 49
1.–10. Answers will vary.

Activity 50
1a. 50/100 or 1/2; b. 10/100 or 1/10; c. 5/100 or 1/20; d. 5/100 or 1/20
2. It would depend on what they got from the machine.
3. 4/66 or 2/33
4. No. Five jawbreakers cost 25¢; buying all the gumballs cost 75¢ more.

Activity 51
1. Trial 1   10/20   10/20
   Trial 2   10/20   10/19
   Trial 3   10/20   10/18
   Trial 4   10/20   10/17
2. 9/19
3. Yes.

Activity 52
1. Is the name drawn first replaced for the second draw?
2. It means there is a chance you could win both prizes.
3a. 1/20; b. 1/20
4a. 1/20; b. 1/20
5. If replacement is allowed.
6. 1/20 × 1/20 = 1/400

Activity 53
1. You need to know the number of students in your grade level 1–3 or 4–6 in the city; and the number of students in your school K–6.
2. Ask the school secretary or school superintendent.
3. Answers will vary by school and city.

Activity 54
1. HHH HHT HTH HTT
   THH THT TTH TTT
2. 8
3. Yes.
4. 1/8
5. 6/8
6. 1/8
7. No.
8. Linda
9. No.
10. Give Vicki and Dan 6 points each time they win.

Activity 55
1. 8
2. HHH HHT HTH HTT
   THH THT TTH TTT
3. 16
4. HHHH HHHT HHTH HHTT
   HTHH HTHT HTTH HTTT
   THHH THHT THTH THTT
   TTHH TTHT TTTH TTTT
5a. 1/16; b. 6/16 or 3/8;
  c. 4/16 or 1/4; d. 1/16;
  e. 15/16; f. 1/16
6. 32
7a. 64; b. 1/64
8. Yes, they are powers of 2.
9. Yes.

Activity 56
1. 16
2. 1/16
3a. 2; b. 4; c. 5
4a. 5; b. 20; c. 30;
  d. 20; e. 5
5.–10. Answers will vary.

Activity 57
1.–5. Answers will vary.

Activity 58
1. Table should read:
11	12	13	14	15	16
21	22	23	24	25	26
31	32	33	34	35	36
41	42	43	44	45	46
51	52	53	54	55	56
61	62	63	64	65	66
2. 12
3. 12/36 or 1/3
4. 18/36 or 1/2
5. 6/36 or 1/6
6. 18/36 or 1/2
7. 9/36 or 1/4
8. 11, 13, 23, 31, 41, 43, 53, 61
9. 8/36 or 2/9
10. 9/36 or 1/4;   22, 23, 25, 32, 33, 35, 52, 53, 55
11. 11/36
12. 6/36 or 1/6

Activity 59
1. 120
2. You have to roll a 10, 11, or 12 on the dodecahedron.
3. 30
4. 30/120 or 1/4
5. No.
6. Answers will vary.

Activity 60
1.–4. Answers will vary.

Activity 61
1. 5/9
2. 4/9
3. 3/9 or 1/3
4. 1/9
5. 4/9

Activity 62
1. 70%
2a. 3;   3 is 30% of 10;
   b. No; 4 is not too far from 3.
3. Answers will vary.
4a. No; if the chance of rain is 5%, it should rain on the average 1 day out of 20;
   b. No; his prediction was correct for the 20 day period.
   c.–d. Answers will vary.

Activity 63
1. RRGG   RGRG   RGGR
   GGRR   GRGR   GRRG
2. 5/6
3. 5/6

4. 3/6 or 1/2
5. 2/6 or 1/3
6.–8. Answers will vary.

Activity 64
1. 9
2. 6
3. 54
4. 3/9 or 1/3
5. 2/6 or 1/3
6. 2/9
7. 1
8. 2
9. 2/54 or 1/27
10. Depends on her choice.
11. 6/77

Activity 65
1a. 2;   b. 4
2.   IA   IB   IC   ID
     IIA   IIB   IIC   IID
3. 8
4. 1/8
5. 1/8
6. 8
7. If you roll a 1, choose Road A; a 2, Road B; a 3; Road C; a 4, Road D.
8.–9. Answers will vary.

Activity 66
1. 6/12 or 1/2
2. 5/12
3. 2/12 or 1/6
4. 4/12 or 1/3
5. 10/12 or 5/6
6. 1/12
7. 144
8. 1+6, 6+1, 2+5, 5+2, 3+4, 4+3
9a. 24;   b. 2
10. Yes.
11. No.
12a. 13; it has the most ways to occur;   b. 2 and 24; there is only one way for each of these to occur
13. 6/144 or 1/24
14. 72/144 or 1/2
15. 50/144 or 25/72
16. 114/144 or 57/72

Activity 67
1. Most students will say 13.
2.–4. Answers will vary. The real average is 9.6 cards *before* the first ace.

Activity 68
1. Most students will say 5.
2. 10
3.–4. Answers will vary.

Activity 69
1.–7. Answers will vary.

Activity 70
1.–3. Answers will vary.
4. Roll the dice more times.
5. Find the number of ways each sum can be rolled, divide that number by 216, and write the answer as a three-place decimal.

Activity 71
1.–2. Answers will vary.
3. B
4.
111	211	311
112	212	312
113	213	313
121	221	321
122	222	322
123	223	323
131	231	331
132	232	332
133	233	333
5a. 3/27 or 1/9;   b. 18/27 or 2/3; c. 6/27 or 2/9
6. Give Player A 6 points for each win; Player B 1 point for each win, and Player C 3 points for each win.

Activity 72
1.–2. Answers will vary.
3. The guess should be better after drawing without replacement.
4. It would be harder to make the estimate with 10.
5. The more selections, the closer the experimental probability should be to the theoretical.
6. Answers will vary.

Activity 73
1. Answers will vary.
2. Yes.
3. Yes.
4. There are 36 possible outcomes from rolling two dice. Six of them are doubles. The probability of rolling a double is 6/36 or 1/6. Thus, on the average, every sixth roll will be a double.